A BIBLIOGRAPHY ON JUDAISM &

JEWISH-CHRISTIAN RELATIONS

A selected, annotated listing of works on Jewish faith and life, and the Jewish-Christian encounter. Compiled by Max Celnik, M.L.S. and Isaac Celnik, M.H.L.

Anti-Defamation League of B'nai B'rith
315 Lexington Avenue, New York, N.Y. 10016

5725

Preface

My work over the years with Christian educators, writers and editors has made clear the need for a bibliography of the kind presented here. This selected, annotated listing aims to serve as a convenient guide to currently obtainable books in two basic areas of study, seen mainly from the Jewish perspective: (1) Judaism, its history, literature, beliefs, practices and institutions; and 2) the Christian-Jewish encounter, from its origins to the present time.

For maximum practicality and usefulness to scholar and layman alike, we have limited our final choice of volumes to just under 300. Despite the obvious merit of a great many authoritative works written by Christian scholars in these subject areas, they have generally not been included, since our primary objective is to supply a collection of titles representing various Jewish viewpoints.

Our thanks go to Max and Isaac Celnik for their expert preparation of this manuscript.

We are grateful to a group of distinguished Jewish, Protestant and Roman Catholic scholars and librarians to whom we submitted this manuscript before publication. Their invaluable comments, criticisms and suggestions were very carefully considered, and many recommendations were incorporated in the final text. We also want to express our appreciation for their gracious words of commendation.

RABBI SOLOMON S. BERNARDS, Director
Department of Interreligious Cooperation

TABLE OF CONTENTS

"I am delighted to know that it [the Bibliography] will soon be published. Christian students will find the sections from IV to XIX especially valuable, for even those of them who are well acquainted with literature dealing with the Old Testament are often relatively unfamiliar with that of post-biblical Judaism. This bibliography will surely be welcomed by them."

MSGR. MYLES BOURKE
Dean of Studies
St. Joseph's Seminary

"It should prove most helpful to students and clergymen who desire readily available material on this subject. The subject divisions of the titles are scholarly enough to lead to the literature in depth, but not so technical as to confuse the student who has no previous knowledge of the field."

DR. GEORGE H. BRICKER
Vice President
American Theological Library Association

"...This should prove to be a valuable contribution to scholars and others interested in Judaism and Jewish-Christian relations. I hope it leads many to reading in this area and so gradually deepen our understanding."

REV. BERNARD COOKE, S.J.
Professor of Theology
Marquette University

"I think that this bibliography will be an important contribution to bibliography on Jews and Judaism and I hope it will receive wide distribution."

MR. JACOB I. DIENSTAG
Librarian, Mendel Gottesman Library
Yeshiva University

"Your bibliography is a superb selection and will prove most useful, I am sure."

DR. FREDERICK GRANT
Emeritus Professor of
Biblical Theology
Union Theological Seminary

"...I hope that the bibliography will find a large circulation and that it will be used widely."

REV. RONAN HOFFMAN, O.F.M. Conv.
The School of Sacred Theology
The Catholic University of America

"This is an important contribution. We are grateful that you plan to publish it....I find that, in general, it is well done, responsible, and constructive, in view of the purposes for which it is to be issued."

DR. RAYMOND P. MORRIS
Librarian
Yale Divinity School

"I have perused the Bibliography with a great deal of interest and appreciation. There is a wealth of resource material itemized here that should prove of great help precisely for those for whom it is intended; namely, teachers of religion in Christian churches and schools whose knowledge of all history, let alone Jewish history, is often quite limited. This publication...should open up an entirely new world to these people. The brief description of each item...is also excellent as a means of making people select more wisely the items that will give them specific and immediate help...congratulations on an excellent and timely work."

DR. COERT RYLAARSDAM
Professor of Old Testament
The University of Chicago
Divinity School

"I regard it as a very important and useful piece of work, and I hope that it will find wide use in the country."

MR. MENAHEM SCHMELCZER
Associate Librarian
Library of the Jewish
Theological Seminary

"I have read it with interest and appreciation. The information it contains will be very useful to the wide body of people for which it is intended. I want you to send me a copy when it is published, for I am sure that I need it.... Let me congratulate you upon the preparation of this publication."

DR. LUTHER A. WEIGLE
Chairman
The Standard Bible Committee;
Dean Emeritus
Yale Divinity School

Introduction

I. For Whom Is This Bibliography Intended?
A. Writers and editors of Christian education textbooks, workbooks, teachers' guides and curricula of religious instruction.

B. Faculty and students of theological seminaries, and of university departments of religion, Semitics, Judaic studies, and world culture.

C. Clergymen, directors of religious education and teachers in Sunday and parochial school systems.

D. Public libraries, and libraries of seminaries, universities, colleges, high schools, churches, synagogues, and community organizations.

E. Christian and Jewish laymen who are interested in the history, background and future of Judaism and Jewish-Christian relations, and those who wish to build a basic library in Judaica.

II. What This Bibliography Contains
A. Works by Jewish authors which reflect a wide spectrum of views.

B. Each work included is available through standard retail outlets and/or general libraries. Works out of print and unavailable have not been included.

C. Each title is annotated with one or two descriptive sentences.

D. Complete data as to the author, publisher, year of publication and availability of a paperback edition is provided.

E. For the reader's convenience, a partial list of public, university and Jewish-sponsored libraries where these works can be obtained is included. Also appended is a list of Jewish periodicals in which scholarly and popular presentations of problems of Jewish concern are to be found, as well as reviews of the latest Jewish books. Other appendices include the addresses of all publishers represented herein and an index by title and author of all volumes included.

III. Acknowledgement
The editors gratefully acknowledge the excellent and patient service of the following libraries in New York City: The Jewish Division, New York Public Library; The Jewish Theological Seminary Library; Yeshiva University libraries; The Hebrew Union College-Jewish Institute of Religion Library.

The assistance of the director of the Department of Interreligious Cooperation of ADL, Rabbi Solomon S. Bernards, proved invaluable in the preparation of this bibliography.

IV. About the Editors

Max Celnik has an M.L.S. from Rutgers University Graduate School of Library Service and a B.H.L. from the Seminary College of Jewish Studies, Jewish Theological Seminary. He is college librarian at Stern College for Women of Yeshiva University.

Isaac Celnik has an M.H.L. from the School of Judaica, Jewish Theological Seminary.

I. Reference Works

AUSUBEL, N.
Book of Jewish Knowledge
New York: Crown Publishers, 1964.
   A single-volume, handy guide for all those who would like to have basic and precise information about Judaism ready at hand. Serves as a practical and comprehensive digest of Judaica.

BARON, J. L., editor
A Treasury of Jewish Quotations
New York: Crown Publishers, 1956.
   An important reference guide to aphorisms, maxims, and comments of Jewish authorship and/or Jewish themes.

FINE, M. and M. HIMMELFARB, editors
American Jewish Year Book
Philadelphia: American Jewish Committee and Jewish Publication Society, annual publication.
   Authoritative compendium of demographic, civic, political, religious, and cultural data concerning Jews in the United States and around the world. Also contains special articles, directories of Jewish organizations and periodicals, bibliography, necrology, and Jewish calender. Invaluable reference work.

FINKELSTEIN, L., editor
The Jews: Their History, Culture, and Religion; third edition; 2 volumes
New York: Harper and Row, 1960.
   This work contains forty-two essays by leading scholars on: 1. The History of Judaism and the Jews; 2. The Role of Judaism in Civilization; 3. The Sociology and Demography of the Jews; and 4. The Jewish Religion.

HASTINGS, J., editor
Encyclopedia of Religion and Ethics; 13 volumes
New York: Scribner's, 1924-1927.
   An old but still useful comprehensive study of "every religion or custom" and all the great systems of ethics, including "every ethical movement, every philosophical idea, [and] every moral practice."

The Jewish People: Past and Present; 4 volumes
New York: Jewish Encyclopedic Handbooks, 1955.

A collection of monographs on Jewish history, religion, and literature by leading scholars. Volume four, subtitled "300 Years of Jewish Life in the United States," is devoted to the religious, cultural, socio-economic, and national activities of American Jewry, especially in the last three generations.

LANDMAN, I., editor
The Universal Jewish Encyclopedia; 10 volumes
New York: Universal Jewish Encyclopedia Company, 1939-1943.

A popular presentation of Jews and Judaism since the earliest times.

PEARL, C. and R. S. BROOKS
A Guide to Jewish Knowledge
London: Jewish Chronicle Publications, 1956.

A clear, brief guide to the Jewish religion, history, and language, with concise bibliography for further study. Excellent for introductory text and quick reference.

ROTH, C., editor
The Standard Jewish Encyclopedia
Garden City: Doubleday, 1959.

Although comprehensive in scope, this work is "intended basically as a work of contemporary reference," and emphasizes recent Jewish history and scholarship.

SCHNEIDERMAN, H. and I. J. Karpman
Who's Who in World Jewry: A Biographical Dictionary of Outstanding Jews
New York: David McKay, 1965.

An important reference work providing biographical data of prominent contemporary Jews throughout the world.

SINGER, I., managing editor
The Jewish Encyclopedia; 12 volumes
New York: Funk and Wagnalls, 1901-1906. Reprinted—New York: Ktav Publishing, 1963.

A descriptive record of the history, religion, literature, and customs of the Jewish people from earliest times to present day. Prepared under the direction of more than four hundred scholars, this comprehensive work remains the authoritative encyclopedia of Judaica.

STEINBACH, A. A., editor
Jewish Book Annual
New York: Jewish Book Council of America, annual publication.

A fine anthology of articles on current aspects of English, Yiddish, and Hebrew literature. An exhaustive, annotated bibliography of each year's harvest of books in three languages is given.

II. Bible and Biblical Literature

*ALBRIGHT, W. F.
The Biblical Period from Abraham to Ezra: An Historical Survey
New York: Harper and Row, 1963.

A revision and expansion of the essay, "The Biblical Period," which originally appeared in Finkelstein's **The Jews.**

AVI-YONAH, M. and E. G. KRAELING
Our Living Bible
New York: McGraw-Hill, 1962.

A colorfully illustrated work on the significant archaeological discoveries which influence our understanding of the Old and New Testaments. Important for individual and classroom Bible study.

*BAMBERGER, B. J.
The Bible: A Modern Jewish Approach
Washington, D.C.: B'nai B'rith Hillel Foundation, 1955.

A popular explanation of the meaning and relevance of the Bible for modern man.

BEWER, J. A.
The Literature of the Old Testament; third edition, revised
New York: Columbia University Press, 1962.

An historical and interpretative survey of the literature of the Old Testament based on archaeological findings and the work of different schools of biblical criticism.

BLANK, S. H.
Jeremiah: Man and Prophet
New York: Hebrew Union College Press, 1961.

The author presents a portrait of the prophet's life and religious experience and an insight into his prophetic message.

BLANK, S. H.
Prophetic Faith in Isaiah
New York: Harper and Row, 1958.
   A biblical scholar selects significant passages and subjects them to modern biblical criticism. An informative study on the message of the "several Isaiahs."

BRIGHT, J.
The Anchor Bible: Jeremiah
Garden City: Doubleday, 1965.
   Includes a valuable introduction, new translation, and important notes by an eminent Christian Bible scholar.

BRIGHT, J.
A History of Israel
Philadelphia: Westmister Press, 1959.
   An authoritative study of the political and religious facts in the history of the Israelites from the age of the Patriarchs to the period of the Maccabees.

*BUBER, M. (translated from the German by C. Witton-Davies)
The Prophetic Faith
New York: The Macmillan Co., 1949.
   "The task of this book is to describe [the prophetic teaching]... both as regards its historical process and as regards its antecedents. This is the teaching about the relation between the God of Israel and Israel."—Introduction.

*CASPER, B. M.
An Introduction to Jewish Bible Commentary
New York: Thomas Yoseloff, 1960.
   Brief descriptions of the most famous Jewish Bible commentators from ancient times to the present.

CASSUTO, U. (translated from the Hebrew by I. Abrahams)
A Commentary on the Book of Genesis; volumes 1 and 2
Jerusalem: Magnes Press, volume 1: 1961; volume 2: 1964.
   An original and exhaustive commentary on Genesis, based upon an historic-philological method of interpretation.

COHEN, A., editor
Soncino Books of the Bible; 14 volumes
New York: Soncino Press, 1950.

"Designed primarily for the ordinary reader of the Bible," this work provides the Hebrew text with a fine English translation and commentary, which for the most part *"takes into account the exegesis of the Talmudical Rabbis... [and] the leading Jewish commentators."*

CORNFELD, G.
Adam to Daniel: An Illustrated Guide to the Old Testament and Its Background.
New York: The Macmillan Co., 1961.

This product of modern Israeli research and thought gives a concise, well-documented, and illustrated picture of the Bible and the biblical world. Draws upon modern biblical criticism and archaeological findings.

CORNFELD, G.
Daniel to Paul: Jews in Conflict with Graeco-Roman Civilization, History, Religion, etc.
New York: The Macmillan Co., 1962.

A companion volume to **Adam to Daniel,** this work presents a scholarly and readable account of the period up to and beyond the New Testament. Subtitled *"Historical and religious background to the Hasmoneans, Dead Sea Scrolls, the New Testament World, early Christianity, and the Bar Kochba War."*

FINEGAN, J.
Light From the Ancient Past: The Archaeological Background of the Hebrew and the Christian Religion.
Princeton: Princeton University Press, 1959.

Based upon archaeological research of the last one hundred and fifty years, presents the backgrounds of Judaism and Christianity in a study of middle east civilizations from 5,000 B.C.E. to 500 C.E.** Numerous photographs and quotations from ancient sources add to the vividness of the account.

FREEHOF, S. B.
The Book of Psalms: A Commentary
New York: Union of American Hebrew Congregations, 1938.

Intended for the general reader, the translation and commentary make extensive use of the Aramaic transla-

** B.C.E.—Before Common Era; C.E.—Common Era

tion (the Targum), the Septuagint, and the traditional, medieval Jewish commentators.

FREEHOF, S. B.
Preface to Scripture
New York: Union of American Hebrew Congregations, 1950.

Part one answers general questions such as "How the Bible Grew and Was Preserved" and "How Was the Bible Interpreted in the Past?" The second part is devoted to selections from Scripture with a clear commentary. Each part includes questions and bibliography which help make this book useful to adult study classes.

*GINZBERG, L.
Legends of the Bible
Philadelphia: Jewish Publication Society, 1956.

A shorter version of **Legends of the Jews,** originally published in seven volumes. "The task he set before himself was to reproduce the mainstreams and the undercurrents of the biblical Haggadah."—From S. Spiegel's introduction to the 1956 edition. The paperback edition is titled **Legends of the Jews.**

GOLDMAN, S.
The Book of Human Destiny; 2 volumes
Philadelphia and New York: Jewish Publication Society, 1949; Harper and Row, 1948.

The first volume, "The Book of Books," includes an interesting account of several hundred quotations "illustrating the use and misuse to which the Bible has been put" and the Bible's part in stimulating thought and action in all spheres of life. The introduction presents a history of the Hebrew canon and of biblical commentaries, as well as an understanding of modern archaeological research and biblical criticism. The second volume, "In the Beginning," is a commentary on the Book of Genesis and includes a section relating the original interpretations of artists, poets, dramatists, etc.

*GOLDMAN, S.
The Ten Commandments
Chicago: University of Chicago Press, 1956.

This commentary blends ancient, medieval, and modern rabbinic insight with critical interpretations.

*Book available in paperback edition.

*GOODSPEED, E. J., translator
The Apocrypha, an American Translation
New York: Random House, Modern Library Paperback, 1958.

A lucid translation "based directly upon the Greek text."

GORDIS, R.
Koheleth, The Man and His World
New York: Jewish Theological Seminary of America, 1955.

The Hebrew text with translation, commentary, and notes. There is an introductory study of the background of Oriental Wisdom, the nature and content of Hebrew Wisdom Literature, and the language, style, and dating of Koheleth.

HASTINGS, J.
Dictionary of the Bible; revised edition
New York: Scribner's, 1927.

An outstanding dictionary on the Bible, containing authoritative articles on Jewish subjects.

HERTZ, J. H., editor
The Pentateuch and Haftorahs
New York: Oxford University Press, 1929-1936.

Hebrew text with translation. The illuminating commentary provided draws upon Jewish and non-Jewish commentators of both the past and present.

HESCHEL, A. J.
The Prophets
New York: Harper and Row, 1962.

A scholarly, theological understanding of the consciousness of the prophet and the nature of prophecy.

The Holy Scriptures According to the Masoretic Text
Philadelphia: Jewish Publication Society, 1917.

This English translation of the Scriptures "aims to combine the spirit of Jewish tradition with the results of biblical scholarship, ancient, medieval, and modern."

KASHER, M. M. (translated from the Hebrew under the editorship of H. Freedman)
Encyclopedia of Biblical Interpretation
New York: American Biblical Encyclopedia Society, 1953.

Presents the text of the Pentateuch with commentary and interpretations culled from the Talmud and Midrash.

This is a condensation of the author's projected 35-volume monumental work in Hebrew: **Torah Shlemah (Complete Torah).** Nine volumes of this work have appeared so far.

KAUFMANN, Y.
(translated from the Hebrew by M. Greenberg)
The Religion of Israel
Chicago: University of Chicago Press, 1960.
   A translation and abridgement of Kaufmann's eight volume work, **History of the Israelite Religion.** Deals with the history, nature, and literature of the Israelite religion of the pre-exilic age.

MAY, H. G.
Oxford Bible Atlas
New York: Oxford University Press, 1962.
   Important reference work providing physical maps, archaeological maps, and historical maps of the Old Testament, Apocrypha and New Testament periods. Included is an essay, "Archaeology and the Bible" by R. W. Hamilton.

*NEHER, A. (translated from the French by I. Marinoff)
Moses and the Vocation of the Jewish People
New York: Harper and Row, 1959.
   Discusses the historical Moses, his calling, "the vocation of the Jewish people," and "the faith kept by the Jewish people with Moses." A study of the origins and development of the Jewish faith.

NOTH, M. (translated from the German by S. Godman)
History of Israel; second edition
New York: Harper and Row, 1960.
   A first rate, detailed treatment of the origin of ancient Israel. It covers the history of the Jewish people from the settlement of the Twelve Tribes to the revolt of Bar-Kochba and the early phases of Judaism and Christianity.

*ORLINSKY, H. M.
Ancient Israel; second edition
Ithaca: Cornell University, 1960.
   A history of the Jewish tradition from its origin in the Fertile Crescent through the Babylonian Exile and the restoration of Judah.

*Book available in paperback edition.

PFEIFFER, R. H.
Introduction to the Old Testament
New York: Harper and Row, 1948.

A significant study of the historical background, thought, and style of the Hebrew Bible. Divided into five parts: 1. The Old Testament as a Whole; 2. The Pentateuch; 3. The Former Prophets; 4. The Latter Prophets; and 5. The Hagiographa.

PRITCHARD, J. B.
The Ancient Near Eastern Texts Relating to the Old Testament; second edition
Princeton: Princeton University Press, 1954.

A fine anthology of ancient near eastern texts important for an understanding of the Old Testament. These include, among others, legal and historical sources and texts concerning the rituals, festivals, and prayers of ancient cultures and civilizations.

SANDMEL, S.
The Hebrew Scriptures—An Introduction to Their Literature and Religious Ideas
New York: Alfred A. Knopf, 1963.

A non-technical introduction and summary of each of the books of the Hebrew Bible, discussing, also, their impact on both Judaism and Christianity.

SILVER, A. H.
Moses and the Original Torah
New York: The Macmillan Co., 1949.

An interesting attempt to explain the inner contradictions of the Bible by an understanding of the theological differences between the northern and southern Kingdoms of Israel.

SPEISER, E. A.
The Anchor Bible: Genesis
Garden City: Doubleday, 1964.

A fine introduction, fresh translation, and valuable notes by a distinguished Jewish Bible scholar.

The Torah: The Five Books of Moses
Philadelphia: Jewish Publication Society, 1963.

A readable, scholarly translation of the Five Books of Moses, which takes into account the "significant advances made during the past half century in biblical archaeology and...the recovery of the languages and civilizations of the peoples among whom the Israelites lived and whose modes of living and thinking they largely shared."

New translations of the Prophets and Writings are currently in preparation.

VAUX, R. de (translated from the French by J. McHugh)
Ancient Israel, Its Life and Institutions
New York: McGraw-Hill, 1961.

An interesting, well researched presentation of the family, civil, military, and religious institutions of the people of Israel in Old Testament times. There is an introductory study of nomadism and tribal organization.

*WRIGHT, G. E.
Biblical Archaeology; revised edition
Philadelphia: Westminster Press, 1963.

"The purpose of this volume is to summarize the archaeological discoveries which directly illumine biblical history, in order that the Bible's setting in the ancient world and its relation to its environment may be more readily comprehended."—From the Foreword.

III. Judaism and Christianity

*BAECK, L. (translated from the German by W. Kauffmann)
Judaism and Christianity
Philadelphia: Jewish Publication Society, 1958.

Five scholarly essays on the different attitudes and institutions of the two religions. Included are essays on "The Faith of Paul" and "The Gospel as a Document of the History of the Jewish Faith."

*BUBER, M. (translated from the German by N. P. Goldhawk)
Two Types of Faith: The Interpenetration of Judaism and Christianity
New York: Harper and Row, 1961.

A theological inquiry into Pharisaic Judaism and early Christianity presenting the differences and similarities of the two types of faith and their contents.

DAUBE, D.
The New Testament and Rabbinic Judaism
London: University of London, 1956.

*Book available in paperback edition.

A discussion of old and new problems relating to the Rabbinic background of the New Testament, as suggested by parallel and quasi-parallel passages.

FINKELSTEIN, L.
The Pharisees: The Sociological Background of Their Faith; 2 volumes; revised edition
Philadelphia: Jewish Publication Society, 1962.

An original, sociological interpretation of the origin, background, ideals, and legislation of the Pharisees.

GOLDSTEIN, M.
Jesus in the Jewish Tradition
New York: The Macmillan Co., 1950.

An exposition of Jewish literary sources, principally Talmudic, which pertain to Jesus, his life and influence.

GRANT, F. C.
Ancient Judaism and the New Testament
New York: The Macmillan Co., 1959.

The major thesis of this work is that "one cannot truly understand the New Testament or the religion it enshrines without a deep and sympathetic understanding of Judaism." The author explores the Jewish orientation of the New Testament.

GREENSTONE, J.
The Messiah Idea in Jewish History
Philadelphia: Jewish Publication Society, 1948.

A popular outline of the development of the "messiah idea" from biblical times through the modern era with special emphasis on the effect of the historical background on the nature of this ideal.

KLAUSNER, J.
Jesus of Nazareth
New York: The Macmillan Co., 1953.

A noted Jewish scholar retells the life of Jesus in the light of the historical, religious, and socio-economic background of his time.

*KLAUSNER, J. (translated from the Hebrew by W. F. Stinespring)
From Jesus to Paul
New York: The Macmillan Co., 1943. Boston: Beacon, 1960.

An approach to the rise of Christianity set against the

background of the pagan and Jewish thought of the time. This work gives the reader an understanding of both the common grounds of Judaism and Christianity and the issues which divide them.

KLAUSNER, J. (translated from the Hebrew by W. F. Stinespring)
The Messianic Idea in Israel, From its Beginning to the Completion of the Mishnah
New York: The Macmillan Co., 1955.
An historical survey of the messianic idea in: The Period of the Prophets; The Books of the Apocrypha and Pseudepigrapha; and The Period of the Tannaim.

PARKES, J.
Foundations of Judaism and Christianity
Chicago: Quadrangle Books, 1960.
The author, a Christian scholar, writes with sympathetic understanding in a balanced, passionate earnestness of the common foundations of Judaism and Christianity.

PHILO. (translated from the Greek by F. S. Colson and G. H. Whitaker)
[The Writings of] Philo; 10 volumes and 2 supplementary volumes; revised edition
Cambridge, Mass.: Harvard University Press, 1929-1962.
These volumes of the Loeb Classical Library provide the English reader with an excellent translation of the works of "the Jew of Alexandria." The Greek text is included.

SANDMEL, S.
The Genius of Paul—A Study in History
New York: Farrar, Straus and Giroux, 1958.
A study of Paul's teachings in the light of his Jewish background.

*SANDMEL, S.
A Jewish Understanding of the New Testament
New York: Hebrew Union College Press, 1956. New York: University, 1960.
An engaging study of the literature of the New Testament, preceded by analysis of the historical circumstances and background of the era. Concludes with a section devoted to the significance of the New Testament.

*Book available in paperback edition.

SANDMEL, S.
We Jews and Jesus
New York: Oxford University Press, 1965.

A non-technical, informed book on the what and why of the Jewish attitude toward Jesus. Reviews the premodern Jewish approaches and discusses the subject anew in the light of 19th and 20th century scholarship and the recent growth of interreligious understanding.

SCHOEPS, H. J. (translated from the German by D. E. Green)
The Christian Jewish Argument: A History of Theologies in Conflict; third edition
New York: Holt, Rinehart and Winston, 1963.

A stimulating account of the theological controversies of Judaism and Christianity, from those of the Church Fathers and the Rabbis of the early Talmudic Period through the twentieth century debates of Karl Schmidt and Martin Buber.

SCHOEPS, H. J. (translated from the German by H. Knight)
Paul: The Theology of the Apostle in the Light of Jewish Religious History
Philadelphia: Westminster Press, 1961.

A comprehensive, scholarly study of Pauline theology by a Jew "who also wishes to do justice to the Judaism, whence Paul sprang." Among the subjects discussed are: 1. The Eschatology of the Apostle Paul; 2. Paul's Teaching About the Laws; and 3. Perspectives of the History of Religion in Paulinism.

✻SILVER, A. H.
A History of Messianic Speculation in Israel from the First Through the Seventeenth Centuries
New York: The Macmillan Co., 1927. Boston: Beacon, 1959.

A scholarly discussion of messianism and especially messianic calculations from the Talmudic Period until the days of Sabbatai Zvi. A new preface includes the author's comments on the creation of the State of Israel in the light of his theme.

SILVER, A. H.
Where Judaism Differed: An Inquiry into the Distinctiveness of Judaism.
Philadelphia: Jewish Publication Society, 1957.

A well written statement of the great insights and ethical teachings of Judaism by a leading Jewish spokesman of the 20th century. Among the subjects discussed are social progress, equality, freedom, and death.

WINTER, P.
On The Trial of Jesus
Berlin: Walter D. E. Gruyter & Co., 1961.

A critical evaluation by a European Jewish scholar of aspects of the Gospel accounts of the arrest, trial, and crucifixion of Jesus.

WOLFSON, H. A.
Philo: Foundations of Religious Philosophy in Judaism, Christianity, and Islam; 2 volumes
Cambridge, Mass.: Harvard University Press, 1947.

A scholarly treatment of the philosophy of Philo and its growth and development in the succeeding seventeen centuries, with an understanding of the effect of Philonic philosophy on the religious philosophy of three faiths.

ZEITLIN, S.
Who Crucified Jesus?
New York: Bloch Publishing Co., 1964.

An historical study of the background and developments of the first century of this era. "The major thesis of this book is that neither the modern Jew nor his ancestors were responsible in any way whatsoever for the death of Jesus."

IV. Talmudic Literature

BLACKMAN, P., translator
Mishnayoth; 7 volumes
London: Mishna Press, 1951-1956.

Hebrew text with English translation, commentary, and notes. The seventh volume is a valuable supplement and index to the work and provides an important study of the "Grammar of the Talmud" and "On the Importance of the Mishnah Throughout the Ages."

*BOKSER, B. Z.
The Wisdom of the Talmud
New York: Philosophical Library, 1951.

An interesting evaluation of the Talmud from literary

*Book available in paperback edition.

and historical viewpoints. The author discusses the jurisprudence, theology, personal morality, and social ethics of the Talmud.

DANBY, H., editor and translator from the Hebrew
The Mishnah
New York: Clarendon Press, 1933.
　　The standard English translation of the text with brief explanatory notes and an introduction on the purpose, character, origin, and development of the Mishnah.

EPSTEIN, I., editor
The Babylonian Talmud; 18 volumes
New York: Soncino Press, 1961.
　　An almost literal translation of the Talmud with helpful notes. The eighteenth volume provides an index and glossary for this work.

FREEDMAN, H. and M. SIMON, editors
Midrash Rabbah; 10 volumes
New York: Soncino Press, 1939.
　　English translation of this Midrashic text (non-legal, rabbinic literature) with terse, explanatory notes.

*GLATZER, N.
Hammer on the Rock: A Midrash Reader
New York: Schocken, 1962.
　　A brief selection of the non-legal literature of the Talmud and Midrash which aims to present "some of the more succinct, imaginative and eloquent examples of talmudic-midrashic thinking and living." Valuable introductory Midrashic text.

*GOLDIN, J.
The Living Talmud: The Wisdom of the Fathers and its Classical Commentaries.
New York: Mentor, 1957.
　　An excellent translation of the Talmudic treatise "The Wisdom of the Fathers" with selections of the traditional, classical commentaries of Maimonides, Duran, Bertinoro, and others. The author has also provided an illuminating essay, "On the Talmud," introducing the English reader to Talmudic literature.

*HERFORD, R. T., translator, editor and commentator
Pirke Aboth—The Ethics of the Talmud: Sayings of the Fathers

New York: Schocken, 1962.

A fine translation with commentary, noted for its systematic treatment, lucid exposition, and historical notes. Ideal for the student and teacher of Rabbinic literature and ethics.

*MONTEFIORE, C. G. and H. M. LOEWE
Rabbinic Anthology
Philadelphia: Jewish Publication Society, 1960.

An anthology of the religious conceptions of Rabbinic literature. Among the many sections the reader will find of interest are: The Law; Prayer; Justice; and The Family. Included is an essay on "Rabbinical and Early Christian Ethics" by R. H. Snape.

*SCHECHTER, S.
Some Aspects of Rabbinic Theology
New York: Schocken, 1961.

"The task I set myself was to give a presentation of Rabbinic opinion on a number of theological topics as offered by the Rabbinic literature." Among the subjects discussed are "Election of Israel," "The Law," "Sin as Rebellion," and "Repentance."

STEWART, R. A.
Rabbinic Theology
London: Oliver and Boyd, 1961.

A Christian scholar's appraisal of living theological issues as seen through Rabbinic literature—God, the Messiah, sin, atonement, immortality, the Rabbinic estimate of man.

*STRACK, H. L. (translated from the German)
Introduction to the Talmud and Midrash; fifth edition
Philadelphia and Cleveland: Jewish Publication Society and Meridian, 1960.

Originally published in 1887, this comprehensive work remains the standard, authoritative text on the Talmud and Midrash, their literature and authors.

V. Philosophy and Religion

AGUS, J. B.
The Evolution of Jewish Thought
New York: Abelard-Schuman, 1959.

A comprehensive exposition of Jewish tradition and

thought designed for the more advanced student of Judaism and general history.

*BAECK, L. (translated from the German by V. Grubwieser and L. Pearl)
The Essence of Judaism
New York: Schocken, 1961.

Originally published in 1905, this work remains one of the widely acclaimed studies of the nature of the underlying ideas of Judaism and their historical development.

BELKIN, S.
Essays in Traditional Jewish Thought
New York: Philosophical Library, 1956.

A collection of the papers dealing with present day problems in the light of traditional Judaism, by a prominent Orthodox leader and thinker. Included are essays on "Traditional Judaism in America" and "The Jewish Community in a Non-Jewish World."

BELKIN, S.
In His Image
New York: Abelard-Schuman, 1961.

An Orthodox scholar's approach to Rabbinic concepts and theology, which he bases on the principles of the sovereignty of God and the sacredness of the individual.

*BERGMAN, S. H.
Faith and Reason: An Introduction to Modern Jewish Thought
New York: Schocken, 1963.

A comprehensible treatment of the thought of such modern Jewish philosophers as Cohen, Rosenzweig, Buber, and Kook, with an emphasis on their approach to the problem of resolving the opposing forces of faith and reason.

BIRNBAUM, P., editor
A Treasury of Judaism
New York: Hebrew Publishing Co., 1957.

An excellent anthology of "some seventy Jewish classics covering a period of thirty centuries" and dealing with the ethical foundations of Judaism. The selections range from biblical texts through the twentieth century writings of Hirsch and Kook.

BLAU, J. L.
The Story of Jewish Philosophy
New York: Random House, 1962.

A clear, concise introduction for the layman to the history of Jewish thought from the Bible through modern times, and the historical circumstances in the development of Jewish philosophy.

BOKSER, B. Z.
Judaism: Portrait of a Faith
New York: Alfred A. Knopf, 1963.

An articulate, scholarly interpretation by a Conservative rabbi of the fundamental concepts of Judaism based upon the classical and modern Jewish writings. Among the thirteen essays are "The Messianic Hope," "The Ethical Imperative," and "Rites and Values."

*****BUBER, M.** (translated from the German by R. G. Smith)
I and Thou
New York: Scribner's, 1960.

An eloquent presentation of Buber's conception of the nature of the experience and relationship of man with other men, with "the Eternal Thou," and with animals and inanimate objects.

BURROWS, M.
The Dead Sea Scrolls
New York: Viking, 1956.

A complete, clearly and simply written volume by the former Director of the American School of Oriental Research of Jerusalem on the archaeological find of the 20th century. Extensive translations from four of the scrolls are available to the reader.

BURROWS, M.
More Light on the Dead Sea Scrolls
New York: Viking, 1958.

A distinguished scholar discusses in detail the many theories pertaining to the origin of this important archaeological treasure. Included are new scrolls and new interpretations.

*Book available in paperback edition.

*CROSS, F. M., JR.
The Ancient Library of Qumran and Modern Biblical Studies; revised edition
Garden City: Doubleday, 1961.

A good all-around introduction to the Dead Sea Scrolls presented in a most interesting manner for both scholar and layman. Excellent maps and photographs enhance this small volume.

DIAMOND, M. L.
Martin Buber—Jewish Existentialist
New York: Oxford University Press, 1960.

An interesting analysis of the philosophy of Buber. Among the subjects discussed and clarified are "I and Thou," "Hasidism," and "The Jewish Jesus."

*EPSTEIN, I.
Judaism: A Historical Presentation
Baltimore: Penguin, 1959.

This work, written from an Orthodox viewpoint, traces the origin and development of the beliefs and doctrines of Judaism as they were shaped in the 4,000 years of Jewish history.

*FINKELSTEIN, L.
The Beliefs and Practices of Judaism
New York: Devin-Adair Co., 1952.

A brief survey and interpretation of the basic values, concepts, and rituals of Judaism, written by a leading spokesman of Conservative Judaism.

*GLATZER, N.
Franz Rosenzweig: His Life and Thought
New York: Schocken, 1961.

A perceptive presentation of Rosenzweig's life and an understanding of his thought. Rosenzweig's philosophy of the Scriptures, of God and man, of the Jewish people and of Zion are clearly analyzed.

GORDIS, R.
The Root and the Branch, Judaism and The Free Society
Chicago: University of Chicago Press, 1962.

An informative discussion of the insights of Judaism and the Jewish tradition in the area of intergroup relations, church and state, education, politics, and international relations.

GUTTMAN, J. (translated from the German by D. W. Silverman)
Philosophies of Judaism: The History of Jewish Philosophy from Biblical Times to Franz Rosenzweig
Philadelphia: Jewish Publication Society, 1964.

A scholarly and lucidly presented appreciation of the significant philosophical documents and movements in Jewish history from biblical through modern times.

*HERTZBERG, A.
Judaism
New York: George Braziller, 1962; Washington Square, 1963.

A conceptual anthology of Jewish literature dealing with the basic values of Judaism. Among others, there are sections on: 1. The Jewish People 2. God 3. Torah 4. Land 5. Doctrine.

HESCHEL, A. J. (F. A. Rothschild, editor)
Between God and Man: An Interpretation of Judaism
New York: Harper and Row, 1959.

A selection of Professor Heschel's writings presenting the substance of the philosopher's understanding of Judaism and the Jewish tradition. The editor has also provided an introductory essay which the reader will find useful and illuminating.

*HESCHEL, A. J.
God in Search of Man
Philadelphia: Jewish Publication Society, 1963.

A major theological, philosophical statement by an eminent Jewish theologian.

HIRSCH, S. R. (translated from the German by I. Grunfeld)
Horeb, A Philosophy of Jewish Laws and Observances;
2 volumes
New York: Soncino Press, 1962.

In these two volumes, a venerated leader of 19th century European Orthodoxy calls for Jewish Law as the center of Jewish life and thought and examines the fundamental principles of Torah under the headings of: 1. Teachings, Judgements, and Statutes; 2. Commandments and Religious Duties; 3. Symbols of Word and Deed; and 4. Divine Service.

*Book available in paperback edition.

*HUSIK, I.
A History of Medieval Jewish Philosophy
New York: The Macmillan Co., 1946.

This classic presentation of the history of medieval Jewish philosophy includes analyses of the works of Ibn Gabirol, Judah Halevi, Ibn Daud, Maimonides, Hasdai Crescas, and Joseph Albo. The introductory essay will prove illuminating to the reader.

KADUSHIN, M.
The Rabbinic Mind
New York: The Jewish Theological Seminary of America, 1965.

A philosophical analysis of the Rabbinic mind as evident from Hagaddic and Halakhic sources. This volume "discusses such problems as the transmission of social values, the integration of the self, [and] the relation of the self to society."

KAPLAN, M. M.
Judaism as a Civilization
New York: Reconstructionist Press, 1957.

This book gave the initial impetus to the Reconstructionist movement. Offers a program for maintaining the continuity of Jewish civilization in the face of today's challenging conditions.

*MAIMONIDES, M. (translated from the Arabic by M. Friedlander)
The Guide for the Perplexed; second edition
New York: Dover, 1904.

This edition presents the English reader with the great medieval work, written "to thinkers whose studies have brought them into collision with religion." A helpful introductory essay is provided by the editor.

MILLGRAM, A. E., editor
Great Jewish Ideas
Washington, D.C.: B'nai B'rith Department of Adult Jewish Education, 1964.

An interesting collection of seventeen essays on 1. Israel, People of the Covenant; 2. Torah, the Jewish Way of Life; 3. The Jewish Vision of God and Man; and 4. A Tradition of Transition.

MOORE, G. F.
Judaism in the First Centuries of the Christian Era, the Age of the Tannaim; 3 volumes
Cambridge, Mass.: Harvard University Press, 1927-1930.

"The aim of the present work is to exhibit the religious conceptions and moral principles of Judaism, its modes of worship and observance, and its distinctive piety, in the form in which, by the end of the second century, they attained general acceptance and authority." Volume three is devoted to "longer notes and discussions."

POLISH, D.
The Eternal Dissent
New York: Abelard-Schuman, 1959.

A pungent, thoughtful analysis of Judaism as a "faith of dissent" from the idolatries of all times and conditions.

POOL, D. de Sola
Why I Am a Jew
New York: Thomas Nelson, 1957.

An interesting and well written account of the history and traditions of Judaism. The author, in examining the question, "What is a Jew?" discusses, among other subjects, the synagogue, prayer, the Jewish home, The Holy Land, The Chosen People, and the Messiah.

*RINGGREN, H.
The Faith of Qumran; Theology of the Dead Sea Scrolls
Philadelphia: Fortress Press, 1963.

An authoritative account of the doctrines, organization, and cult of the "Dead Sea Community" with an understanding of their place in the history of the world's major religions.

ROTH, C.
Jewish Contributions to Civilization
New York: Union of American Hebrew Congregations, 1940.

After a brief account of Jewish history, the author describes the contribution the Jews have made to Western Civilization in letters, art, music, philosophy, science, medicine, economics, and law.

*Book available in paperback edition.

*ROTH, L.
Jewish Thought as a Factor in Civilization
New York: UNESCO, 1954.

A brief summation of the background and basic ideas of Judaism and their impact on the intellectual and moral heritage of mankind.

*SCHECHTER, S.
Studies in Judaism; series 1-3.
Philadelphia: Jewish Publication Society, 1896-1919.

These collections of Schechter's essays remain standard, scholarly, and superbly readable accounts of Jewish history and thought. Among the many topics with which Schechter deals are: the Hasidim, the history of Jewish tradition, the Bible and the Talmud.

SCHWARZ, L.
Great Ages and Ideas of the Jewish People
New York: Modern Library, 1962.

An excellent anthology of essays by leading Jewish scholars of our time on the history of the Jews and the basic ideas and values that they embraced through the ages. Included is a selected bibliography, which the reader will find useful.

STEINBERG, M. (edited with an introduction by A. Cohen)
Anatomy of Faith
New York: Harcourt, Brace and World, 1960.

A collection of seven essays by an eminent Conservative rabbi with an introductory essay on the life and thought of Steinberg by the editor. Included in the work are "The Theological Issues of the Hour" and "New Currents in Religious Thought."

STEINBERG, M.
Basic Judaism
New York: Harcourt, Brace and World, 1947.

A brief, eloquent, and comprehensive overview of the fundamentals of Judaism and the life of the Jew in his home, synagogue, and among the nations. The Jewish view of Jesus is extensively explored.

TREPP, L.
Eternal Faith, Eternal People: A Journey into Judaism
Englewood Cliffs, N.J.: Prentice-Hall, 1962.

A good introduction to the Jewish faith and to the processes of Jewish history; discusses differences between Judaism and Christianity.

VI. Language

*BEN-YEHUDA, E., editor
Ben-Yehuda's Pocket English-Hebrew, Hebrew-English Dictionary
New York: Washington Square, 1964.

Handy pocket dictionary containing over 30,000 entries. Included are comprehensive but brief explanations of grammar and tables of irregular verbs.

CHOMSKY, W.
Hebrew: The Eternal Language
Philadelphia: Jewish Publication Society, 1957.

This scholarly yet readable biography of the Hebrew language addresses itself to the problems, "How the language began to be spoken," "How the written language took form," "How the language was preserved," and "How the language meets modern needs."

DIRINGER, D.
The Story of the Aleph Beth
New York: Philosophical Library, 1958.

A popular and informative introduction to the origins and development of the Hebrew alphabet.

GROSSMAN, R. (revised and edited by M. H. Segal)
Compendious Hebrew-English Dictionary
Tel Aviv: Dvir Publishing Company, 1956.

"This dictionary is designed to assist the English-speaking reader in his studies of the Hebrew language and literature of all periods, and especially of the Hebrew Bible and of the literature of contemporary Hebrew."

HOROWITZ, E.
How the Hebrew Language Grew
New York: Jewish Education Committee Press, 1961.

An exciting study of the growth and development of the Hebrew language showing "with what ease and facility Hebrew is meeting the linguistic demands of civilized life in this mid-twentieth century."

ROSEN, H. B.
A Textbook of Israeli Hebrew; With an Introduction to the Classical Language
Chicago: University of Chicago Press, 1962.

*Book available in paperback edition.

An excellent, modern, college-level textbook of the Hebrew language, based on a 1,000 words Foundation Word List designed "to enable the student to read moderately difficult Israeli Hebrew, to write, and to converse in acceptable current Hebrew, and to understand less complex passages of classical Hebrew."

VII. Literature

AUSUBEL, N., editor
A Treasury of Jewish Folklore, Stories, Traditions
New York: Crown Publishers, 1958.
An anthology of Jewish myths and parables, stories, and legends contained in Talmudic and Post-Talmudic sources. Included is a section on the religious and folk songs and dances of the Jewish people.

AUSUBEL, N. and M., editors
A Treasury of Jewish Poetry
New York: Crown Publishers, 1957.
A fine anthology of poetry written by Jews. The selections are divided under four main headings: 1. The Spirit of Man, 2. The Jew in the World, 3. God, 4. The Mind of the Jew. Included is a study of Jewish poetry, from the biblical era through modern times.

*****CAPLAN, S. and H. U. RIBALOW,** editors
The Great Jewish Books and Their Influence on History
New York: Washington Square, 1963.
Twelve essays on Jewish classics, from the Bible to the modern Hebrew poet Bialik. Selections and biographical notes are included.

*****HALEVY-LEVIN, Y.**
Israel Argosy: Volumes 1—
New York: Zionist Organization, annual publication.
An annual publication presenting a selection of stories, essays, and poetry from modern Hebrew literature.

LEFTWICH, J., editor and translator
The Golden Peacock; A Worldwide Treasury of Yiddish Poetry
New York: Thomas Yoseloff, 1961.
This eleven hundred page anthology of Yiddish poetry is mainly divided under geographic headings, grouping together the Yiddish poets of Russia, Galicia, America, Poland, Israel, etc. "The finest and most comprehensive

anthology of its kind."—Nathan Ausubel.

LEWISOHN, L., editor
Jewish Short Stories
New York: Behrman House, 1945.

    This limited anthology of ten short stories provides hours of enjoyable reading. Includes selections from the works of Peretz, Sholem Aleichem, Sholem Asch, Israel Zangwill, Ben Hecht, and Howard Fast.

MILLGRAM, A. E.
An Anthology of Medieval Hebrew Literature
New York: Abelard-Schuman, 1962.

    An important selection of medieval Jewish literature. Included are sections dealing with the poetry of the "golden era" of Spain, and the legal, philosophic, mystical and ethical literature of those times.

RIBALOW, M.
The Flowering of Modern Hebrew Literature: A Volume of Literary Evaluation
New York: Twayne Publishers, 1959.

    Essays dealing with leading figures in modern Hebrew Literature—Bialik, Tchernihovski, Shneur, Fishman, Shimoni, Hameiri, and Shalom. An excellent introduction for the English reader to the character and thought of modern Hebrew literature.

RICHMAN, J.
Jewish Wit and Wisdom
New York: Pardes Publishing House, 1952.

    A colorful anthology of Jewish anecdotes, and **bon mots,** reflecting the entire realm of Jewish life.

SCHWARZ, L.
Golden Treasury of Jewish Literature
New York: Holt, Rinehart and Winston, 1937.

    An anthology of legends, parables, poetry, stories, and philosophical essays on Jews and Judaism.

SCHWARZ, L.
Jewish Caravan
New York: Holt, Rinehart and Winston, 1935.

    A collection of short stories of Jewish life from biblical times to the present day.

*Book available in paperback edition.

*SPIEGAL, S.
Hebrew Reborn
Cleveland: World, 1962.
A scholarly but exciting study of "the most significant figures and currents of the new Hebrew literature." Among the authors discussed are Mendelssohn, Krochmal, Berditchewski and Tchernichovski.

WALLENROD, R.
The Literature of Modern Israel
New York: Abelard-Schuman, 1956.
A survey of modern Hebrew literature dating from the First Aliyah (wave of immigration) of 1882-1905 through the present generation. Included is a chapter on Israel in American Hebrew poetry.

WAXMAN, M.
A History of Jewish Literature; 5 volumes; revised and enlarged edition
New York: Thomas Yoseloff, 1960.
A comprehensive guide to the literature of a people through the ages. An important reference work.

*ZABARA, J. (translated from the Hebrew by M. Hadas)
The Book of Delight
New York: Columbia University Press, 1932.
An excellent translation of the 12th century medieval work of a Jew of Barcelona. The fifteen stories told by the author in this work are analyzed in an introductory essay to illustrate the "free interchange of ideas between East and West early in the Middle Ages."

VIII. Law and Customs

COHEN, B.
Law and Tradition in Judaism
New York: Jewish Theological Seminary of America, 1959.
Eight essays on the "philosophy of Jewish religious law from the point of view of Historical-Traditional Judaism." The reader will find especially interesting the essays on "The Shulhan Arukh as a Guide for Religious Practice Today" and "Law and Ethics in the Light of the Jewish Tradition."

*DRESNER, S. H. and S. SIEGEL
The Jewish Dietary Laws
New York: Burning Bush Press, 1959.

This 71 page pamphlet consists of two well-written essays: "Their Meaning for Our Time," in which Rabbi Dresner traces the institution of the dietary laws to its biblical and rabbinic roots, and "A Guide to Observance," in which Rabbi Siegel provides a concise guide to the laws of Kashrut.

FREEHOF, S. B.
The Responsa Literature
Philadelphia: Jewish Publication Society, 1955.
A general description of the origins and development of Responsa Literature and its portrayal of Jewish history.

FREEHOF, S. B.
A Treasury of Responsa
Philadelphia: Jewish Publication Society, 1963.
A fair sampling of this vast branch of Jewish legal writing, "This volume deals with the medieval and modern Responsa Literature dealing with a variety of subjects: proselytes, polygamy, child adoption, modern Sabbath violations, etc."

GANZFRIED, S. (translated from the Hebrew by H. Goldin)
Code of Jewish Law (Kitzur Shulhan Arukh); available in 4 volumes with Hebrew text or in a single volume English translation; revised edition
New York: Hebrew Publishing Company, 1961.
A fine translation of the classic, traditional text of Jewish laws and customs.

*GINZBERG, L.
On Jewish Law and Lore
Philadelphia: Jewish Publication Society, 1955.
A collection of six essays on the life and thought of the Jewish people. This work includes essays entitled: "Jewish Folklore: East and West," "The Significance of the Halachah for Jewish History," and "The Codification of Jewish Law."

HOROWITZ, G.
The Spirit of Jewish Law
New York: Central Book Co., 1953.
This volume, written by a New York lawyer, contains a self-explanatory sub-title: "A brief account of Biblical and Rabbinical Jurisprudence with a Special Note on Jewish Law and the State of Israel."

*Book available in paperback edition.

SMITH, J. M. P.
The Origin and History of Hebrew Law
Chicago: University of Chicago Press, 1931.

This work traces the history of the legislation of the Old Testament, as found in the Decalogue, Covenant Code, Deuteronomic Code, Holiness Code, Ezekiel's Ideal Code, and the Priestly Code. The author also examines the tradition of the Mosaic authorship of the Pentateuch and provides edited translations of the Code of Hammurabi, and the Assyrian and Hittite Codes as parallel ancient legal systems.

IX. Prayer, Rituals and Festivals

*ARZT, M.
Justice and Mercy: Commentary on the Liturgy of the New Year and the Day of Atonement
New York: Holt, Rinehart and Winston, 1963.

An important aid in understanding and appreciating the High Holy Day Liturgy. The Commentary draws from classic and modern sources, which are often quoted verbatim. Recommended reading for laymen and clergy alike.

BARISH, L.
High Holy Day Liturgy
New York: Jonathan David, 1959.

An interesting and informative commentary and analysis of the High Holy Day Liturgy.

GARFIEL, E.
The Service of the Heart: A Guide to the Jewish Prayer Book
New York: Thomas Yoseloff, 1958.

A knowledgeable understanding of the history and concepts of the Prayer Book is presented in this clearly written commentary.

*GASTER, T. H.
Festivals of the Jewish Year: A Modern Interpretation and Guide
Gloucester, Mass.: Peter Smith, 1962.

A scholarly and stimulating study of the origins and evolution of the Jewish festivals, and parallel customs and ceremonies of other peoples in an attempt to uncover the universal ideas behind them.

*GASTER, T. H.
Passover; Its History and Traditions
Boston: Beacon, 1961.

This work "seeks to present to the inquiring layman the full story of what recent research has to say about the true origins of Passover, the parallels to it in various parts of the world and the historical authenticity of the events which it commemorates."

GOODMAN, P.
The Passover Anthology
Philadelphia: Jewish Publication Society, 1961.

An interesting selection of writings on all aspects of the festival of freedom. Included are classical, medieval, and modern writings on the origin and traditions of Passover. The book is divided into four categories: 1. Passover in History 2. Passover in Literature, Art, and Music 3. Passover for Young People 4. Passover Rejoicing.

GOODMAN, P.
The Purim Anthology
Philadelphia: Jewish Publication Society, 1949.

A selection of writings on the origin and traditions of a Jewish holiday, this work is divided into categories similar to those in the "Passover Anthology," mentioned above. The reader will find especially interesting the section dealing with the manner in which Purim is celebrated in many lands.

GOODMAN, P.
Rejoice in Thy Festival: A Treasury of Wisdom, Wit and Humor for the Sabbath and Jewish Holidays
New York: Bloch Publishing Co., 1956.

"The stories presented in this collection reflect the spirit of Jewish holidays and festivals, their historical background, manner of observance and significance."— Preface.

HERTZ, J. H., editor
The Authorized Daily Prayer Book; revised edition
London: Shapiro, Vallentine and Co., 1959.

A fine English translation of the Hebrew text with commentary. In addition, there is an introductory essay on Prayer, the Synagogue, and the Liturgy.

*Book available in paperback edition.

*HESCHEL, A. J.
The Sabbath
The Earth is the Lord's
Philadelphia and Cleveland: Jewish Publication Society and Meridian, 1964.

Two lyrical evocations—the first, of the meaning of the Seventh Day; the second, of the inner life of East European Jews before Hitler.

KASHER, M. M., editor
Israel Passover Haggadah
New York: American Biblical Encyclopedia Society, 1950.

Hebrew text with English translation, and commentary based on Aggadic sources. The rituals and customs of the Seder are explained and there is a section of illustrations of Egyptian monuments and ancient manuscripts relevant to Passover.

KIEVAL, H.
The High Holy Days: A Commentary on the Prayer Book of Rosh Hashonah and Yom Kippur
New York: Burning Bush Press, volume 1: 1959.

A helpful commentary on the liturgy and rituals of the High Holy Days. The first in this two volume series deals specifically with Rosh Hashonah.

MILLGRAM, A. E.
Sabbath, the Day of Delight
Philadelphia: Jewish Publication Society, 1944.

The author provides "a practical guide and handbook for Sabbath observance," and includes selections of "the Sabbath in literature, art and music" of the past and present, and essays on "The Origin and Development of the Sabbath" and "The Jewish Sabbath and the Christian Sunday."

*SCHAUSS, H.
Guide to Jewish Holy Days
New York: Schocken, 1962.

An excellent study of the origins and development of the Jewish festivals and their rituals. This work will prove especially valuable in the adult education classroom.

SOLIS-COHEN, E.
Hanukkah, the Feast of Lights
Philadelphia: Jewish Publication Society, 1937.

A careful selection of essays on the history, tradition,

and significance of Hanukkah. A section on "Hanukkah in Literature" of ancient and modern times is included.

Pamphlet Material

*BERNARDS, S., editor
The Living Heritage Of The High Holy Days
New York: Anti-Defamation League, 1962.

The quality and meaning of Rosh Hashanah and Yom Kippur is interpreted from the Liturgy and the writings of ancient and modern commentators. Discussion topics and project suggestions are included.

*BERNARDS, S., editor
The Living Heritage Of Passover: With An Abridged Passover Haggadah In English
New York: Anti-Defamation League, 1962.

An exposition and analysis of one of the most significant Jewish holidays, with a condensed Seder service. Subjects for classroom discussion, project ideas and a bibliography are appended.

*GILBERT, A. and O. TARCOV
Your Neighbor Celebrates; revised edition
New York: Anti-Defamation League, 1963.

A clear, concise explanation of the major Jewish holidays, their historical origins, ceremonies, and significance. Particularly suitable for teenagers.

*GILBERT, A.
Your Neighbor Worships
New York: Anti-Defamation League, 1959.

Offers a "guided tour" of the synagogue, explaining its history and describing its unique architectural features and major ceremonial objects.

*GREENBERG, D. and S. BERNARDS, editors
The Living Heritage Of Hanukkah
New York: Anti-Defamation League, 1964.

An examination of various interpretations of the historical, religious, and ethical significance of the Festival of Lights, from ancient times to contemporary Israel. Contains selections, model Hanukkah service, poetry, music, and topics for discussion.

*Book available in paperback edition.

X. Hasidism and Mysticism

BUBER, M. (translated from the German by M. Friedman)
Hasidism and Modern Man
New York: Horizon Press, 1958.

The first of Buber's two-volume interpretation of Hasidism entitled "Hasidism and the Way of Man." This work contains six writings on the life and thought of Hasidism. Included are essays on "The Life of the Hasidim: Ecstacy, Service, Intention, Humility" and "Love of God and Love of Neighbor."

BUBER, M. (translated from the German and edited by M. Friedman)
The Origin and Meaning of Hasidism
New York: Horizon Press, 1960.

The second volume of Buber's two-volume comprehensive interpretation of the character of Hasidism, "Hasidism and the Way of Man." This work contains nine essays on the history and nature of Hasidism, including "Spirit and Body of the Hasidic Movement" and "The Place of Hasidism in the History of Religion."

*****BUBER, M.** (translated from the German by O. Marx)
Tales of the Hasidim; 2 volumes
New York: Schocken, 1948.
Vol. 1: The Early Masters; Vol. 2: The Later Masters.

The selection of legends included in these two volumes will permit the reader to enter into and experience the reality and ideals of Hasidism. Excellent introductory essays have been provided for both volumes.

MUELLER, E. (translated from the German by M. Simon)
History of Jewish Mysticism
London: East and West Library, 1946.

A brief but comprehensive account of the development of Jewish mysticism from biblical times through the modern era. The reader will find especially interesting the author's treatment of non-Jewish mysticism in its contact and relationship with Jewish thought.

NEWMAN, L. I.
The Hasidic Anthology: Tales and Teachings of the Hasidim
New York: Schocken, 1963.

The subtitle to the 1934 edition is self-explanatory:

"The parables, folk tales, fables, aphorisms, epigrams, sayings, anecdotes proverbs and exegetical interpretations of the Hasidic masters and disciples; their lore and wisdom." The work is alphabetically arranged under subject headings.

*SCHOLEM, G. G.
Major Trends in Jewish Mysticism
New York: Schocken, 1954.
   The standard, scholarly study of Jewish mysticism. The author analyzes and interprets mystical thought from its earliest period through its latest phases.

*SCHOLEM, G. G., editor
Zohar, The Book of Splendor
New York: Schocken, 1963.
   An excellent selection of passages from the Zohar which give the reader an idea of "the power of contemplative fantasy and creative imagery hidden within the seemingly abstruse thinking of the Kabbalists." An introductory essay on the origin, authorship, and historical setting of the Zohar is included.

XI. Jewish History

AGUS, J. B.
The Meaning of Jewish History; 2 volumes
New York: Abelard-Schuman, 1963.
   An original "reconstruction of the fundamental lines of the Jewish historic evolution."—S. W. Baron. Volume one deals with the ancient period, volume two with the medieval period and the modern world. Christian-Jewish relations are extensively explored.

BARON, S. W.
A Social and Religious History of the Jews; 8 volumes; second edition
New York: Columbia University Press, 1958.
Vol. 1-2: Ancient Times (through the period of the Talmud); Vol. 3-8: Middle Ages (500-1200).
   A comprehensive and authoritative study by the Emeritus Professor of Jewish History, Literature and Institutions of Columbia University. An important reference work.

*Book available in paperback edition.

*DUBNOW, S. (edited by K. S. Pinson)
Nationalism and History: Essays on Old and New Judaism
Cleveland and Philadelphia: Meridian and Jewish Publication Society, 1961.

In this series of essays, Dubnow "developed his philosophy of nationalism and its specific relation to the role of the Jew in the modern world..."—K. S. Pinson. Included are essays entitled "The Significance of Jewish History" and "The Survival of the Jewish People."

*GOODMAN, P. (revised and enlarged by I. Cohen)
A History of the Jews
New York: Dutton, 1959.

Originally published in 1919, this outline of Jewish history is still valuable as an introductory textbook for the young and adults alike.

GRAETZ, H. H.
History of the Jews; 6 volumes
Philadelphia: Jewish Publication Society, 1946.

Originally published at the turn of the century, this monumental work remains today the classic, comprehensive study of Jewish history from its beginnings through 1870. Volume 6 provides a convenient table of Jewish history and an index to the first five volumes.

*MARGOLIS, M. L. and A. MARX
A History of the Jewish People
Philadelphia: Jewish Publication Society, 1927.

A brief but clear outline of Jewish history from its beginnings through 1925 C.E. Excellent work for quick reference.

*ROTH, C.
History of the Jews
New York: Schocken, 1961.

A brief survey of Jewish history from biblical days through the present. May be used as an introductory text of Jewish history.

SPEISER, E. A., editor
At the Dawn of Civilization; volume 1 of World History of the Jewish People
New Brunswick, N.J.: Rutgers University Press, 1965.

Describes the environmental, linguistic, and cultural factors of the beginnings of Jewish history. Provides a background to the biblical history of Israel and lands to the North.

The first of a 20 volume series, written by world authorities under the general editorship of Prof. B. Netanyahu of Dropsie College, on the story of the Jewish people from prehistoric times to the present.

XII. History: Ancient and Medieval

*ABRAHAMS, I.
Jewish Life in the Middle Ages
Cleveland: Meridian, 1960.

Originally published in 1896, this scholarly and readable work still remains the classic presentation of the communal organization and institutions of the medieval Jews, as well as of the social, economic, and religious aspects of their lives.

BAER, Y. F. (translated from the German by L. Schoffman)
History of Jews in Christian Spain; volume 1
Philadelphia: Jewish Publication Society, 1961.

A well grounded, comprehensive study of the history of Spanish Jewry from the end of the eleventh through the end of the fourteenth century.

DUBNOW, S.
(translated from the Russian by I. Friedlander)
History of the Jews in Russia and Poland from the Earliest Times Until the Present Days; 3 volumes
Philadelphia: Jewish Publication Society, 1916-1920.

Vol. 1: From the beginning until 1825. Vol. 2: 1825-1894. Vol. 3: 1894-1914, Bibliography, Index. The classic study of the history of Russian and Polish Jewry.

GLATZER, N. N.
Hillel the Elder: The Emergence of Classical Judaism
Washington, D.C.: B'nai B'rith Hillel Foundation, 1959.

A clearly written historical study of Judaism from the days of Herod the Great through the destruction of the Second Temple, with a special emphasis on the life and thought of Hillel the Elder. This brief but lucid account sheds light on the first pre-Christian century in which "the factors emerged which help explain the Jewish people's passionate loyalty to Judaism..."

*Book available in paperback edition.

*JOSEPHUS, F. (translated from the Greek by W. Whiston)
The Life and Works of Flavius Josephus
New York: Holt, Rinehart and Winston, 1957.

   A one-volume edition of Josephus' historical works "Antiquities of the Jews" and "Wars of the Jews," both of which are invaluable historical sources of classical antiquity.

LEON, H. J.
The Jews of Ancient Rome
Philadelphia: Jewish Publication Society, 1960.

   A solid, well presented study of the Jewish community of ancient Rome which takes into account the latest archaeological research. The many illustrations add to the author's description of the economic, political and religious aspects of their lives.

*MARCUS, J.
The Jew in the Medieval World: A Source Book 315-1791
Cleveland: Meridian, 1960.

   An excellent anthology of source material reflecting "the life of the medieval Jew as seen through the eyes of contemporaries." An important reference work.

ROTH, C.
The Jews in the Renaissance
Philadelphia: Jewish Publication Society, 1959.

   An important study of the Jewish contribution to the Renaissance of Learning and Science and the Renaissance of Art, dealing mainly with the "interaction of two societies and of two cultures," which occurred in Italy.

ROTH, C.
Personalities and Events in Jewish History
Philadelphia: Jewish Publication Society, 1953.

   A collection of 23 essays on various historical subjects such as "The Jew as a European," "Folklore of the Ghetto," "The Origin of the Ghetto," and "Who was Columbus," in which Roth propounds the thesis that Columbus was descended from Spanish Jews.

TCHERIKOVER, A. (translated from the Hebrew by S. Appelbaum)
Hellenistic Civilization and the Jews
Philadelphia: Jewish Publication Society, 1959.

   A scholarly understanding of the history of the Jews from the conquests of Alexander the Great through the

Hasmonean Period. Divided into two parts: 1. Hellenistic Civilization in Palestine; and 2. Hellenistic Civilization in the Diaspora.

ZEITLIN, S.
The Rise and Fall of the Judean State: A Political and Social and Religious History of the Second Commonwealth
Philadelphia: Jewish Publication Society, 1962.

Intended to present a systematic history of the Jewish people from 332 B.C.E. until 135 C.E. This first volume brings the reader through 37 B.C.E. and the last Hasmoneans.

XIII. History: Modern

*AGAR, H.
The Saving Remnant: An Account of Jewish Survival
New York: Compass, 1962.

A stirring account of the history of European Jewry since 1914 and the establishment of the State of Israel as seen through the eyes of the American Jewish Joint Distribution Committee.

BARON, S. W.
Modern Nationalism and Religion; second edition
Cleveland: Meridian, 1960.

An "analysis of the fundamental interrelations between the western and modern nationalism." The eight essays include "Protestant Individualism" and "Jewish Ethnicism."

BLAU, J. L. and S. W. BARON
The Jews of the United States 1790-1840: A Documentary History; 3 volumes
New York: Columbia University Press, 1963.

An excellent fifty-year history of the Jews in the United States and their interrelation with the general American history of that period. Each of the three hundred and thirty-four documents is prefaced by introductory remarks, as is each of the three volumes.

DAVIS, M.
The Emergence of Conservative Judaism: The Historical School in 19th Century America
Philadelphia: Jewish Publication Society, 1963.

*Book available in paperback edition.

An excellent, scholarly, and well presented account of the Historical School of religious thought "from its formative period as an approach to Jewish life and tradition in America until its emergence as the Conservative Movement." An important study of the development of American Jewish life, especially in the religious and educational spheres in the nineteenth century.

ELBOGEN, I.
A Century of Jewish Life
Philadelphia: Jewish Publication Society, 1944.

The standard, authoritative account of Jewish history from 1848-1942. An important quick-reference work.

*GRAYZEL, S.
A History of the Contemporary Jews
Cleveland: Meridian, 1960.

An interesting 179 page account of modern Jewish history from 1900. The reader will find the bibliography very useful for further reading.

HANDLIN, O.
Adventure in Freedom: 300 years of Jewish life in America
New York: McGraw-Hill, 1954.

An interpretation and "retrospective stocktaking" of American Jewish history through 1954 as it has "a bearing upon the present and upon the problems of the future."

*HANDLIN, O.
American Jews: Their Story
New York: Anti-Defamation League, 1958. 48 page pamphlet.

A brief, illustrated history of Jewish life in America from 1654 to the present.

LEARSI, R.
The Jews in America, a History
Cleveland: World, 1954.

This well-written account of the history of American Jewry has become the standard popular work on the subject. Valuable as introductory textbook.

MARCUS, J. R.
Early American Jewry; 2 volumes
Philadelphia: Jewish Publication Society, 1951, 1953.

Vol. 1—The Jews of New York, New England and Canada, 1649-1794. Vol. 2—The Jews of Pennsylvania and the South 1655-1790. A comprehensive account of the history of American Jewry of the colonial and early national periods. Includes important documents of those times.

MENKUS, B., editor
Meet the American Jew
Nashville: Broadman Press, 1963.
Eleven essays by prominent Jewish writers on the religious, cultural, and sociological spectrum of the contemporary Jewish community.

*SACHAR, H.
The Course of Modern Jewish History
New York: Dell, 1963.
An excellent account of Jewish history since the French Revolution against the background of world history and "the influence of non-Jewish factors." This articulate work takes into account the wealth of information provided by modern scholarship and research.

*SCHAPPES, M., editor
A Documentary History of the Jews in the United States, 1654-1875
New York: Citadel, 1950.
The author has provided the reader with one hundred and fifty-nine documents which bear upon an understanding of American Jewish history. Each selection is prefaced by a brief, lucid introduction. An important reference work.

SCHWARTZMAN, S. D.
Reform Judaism in the Making
New York: Union of American Hebrew Congregations, 1955.
A popular, historical account of the rise and development of Reform Judaism. Included are accounts of the organization, principles and practices of modern Reform Judaism.

SKLARE, M.
Conservative Judaism, an American Religious Movement
New York: Free Press, 1955.
A sociological study of Jewish life in America and the

*Book available in paperback edition.

problems of the Jewish religious movements. Emphasizes those of the Conservative movement, in particular.

TCHERIKOWER, E., editor (translated from the Yiddish and revised by A. Antonovsky)
The Early Jewish Labor Movement in the United States
New York: Yivo Institute for Jewish Research, 1961.

An important exposition of the background and context out of which the Jewish labor movement developed and history of the pioneer period of that movement in the second half of the 19th century.

The Nazi Holocaust: 1933—1945

DONAT, A.
The Holocaust Kingdom
New York: Holt, Rinehart and Winston, 1965.

A direct, moving account of the Nazi invasion of Poland and the systematic extermination of the Warsaw Ghetto.

FLENDER, H.
Rescue in Denmark
New York: Simon and Schuster, 1963.

A stirring description of how occupied Denmark rose as a nation to save the Danish Jews from Nazi extermination.

HERSEY, J. R.
The Wall
New York: Alfred A. Knopf, 1950.

A noted author's gripping record of the life and struggle for survival during the last days of the Warsaw Ghetto. After many months on Best Seller lists, this work has achieved the status of a classic.

HILBERG, R.
The Destruction of the European Jews
Chicago: Quadrangle, 1961.

A documentary study based upon painstaking research into primary source material and official records of the German Third Reich's systematic destruction of European Jewry.

PEARLMAN, M.
The Capture and Trial of Adolf Eichmann
New York: Simon and Schuster, 1963.

The author presents a detailed description of the discovery and capture of Hitler's lieutenant, the architect of

Jewish genocide, and an enlightening view of the trial of the century.

POLIAKOV, L. (translated from the French)
Harvest of Hate: The Nazi Program for the Destruction of the Jews of Europe
Syracuse: Syracuse University Press, 1954.

A classic, historical study of the systematic extermination of the Jews in Europe. Gives a country-by-country, year-by-year account of Nazi atrocities culled from diaries and personal documents of Nazi leaders. Includes an extensive bibliography and an introduction by Reinhold Niebuhr.

RINGELBLUM, E. (edited and translated from the Yiddish by J. Sloan)
Notes From the Warsaw Ghetto: The Journal of Emmanuel Ringelblum
New York: McGraw-Hill, 1958.

A day-by-day account of the life of the Warsaw Ghetto inhabitants from September, 1939 to the eve of the Ghetto uprising in April, 1943. The author was a noted historian and the author of four books and innumerable monographs.

SCHWARZ-BART, A.
The Last of the Just
New York: Atheneum, 1960.

A moving account of Jewish persecution from medieval times to Hitler's Germany. The author uses fiction to depict the anguish and suffering of generations of Jews.

WELLS, L. W.
The Janowska Road
New York: Macmillan, 1963.

A dramatic, vivid picture of the author's life in German concentration camps. A personal document of man's inhumanity to man.

WIESEL, E. (translated from the French by S. Becker)
The Town Beyond the Wall
New York: Atheneum, 1964.

The hero of this novel, "the messenger of dead Jews," probes the problem of how to explain the evil in the world and asks how man communicates with his fellow man under indescribable conditions and in moments of personal anguish. The author is a survivor of Nazi extermination camps.

XIV. Israel and Zionism

BADI, J.
Fundamental Laws of the State of Israel
New York: Twayne Publishers, 1961.

A compilation of the major legislation enacted in the State of Israel in the first formative decade of its existence, 1948-1958. This includes the Rabbinical Courts Law, the State Education Law, and the Penal Law Revision which abolished the death penalty for murder.

BEN ZVI, Y.
The Exiled and the Redeemed; revised edition
Philadelphia: Jewish Publication Society, 1961.

A vivid description of the Oriental and North African Jewish communities, their distinctive way of life, and the story of their return to the State of Israel.

DAVIS, M., editor
Israel: Its Role in Civilization
New York: Jewish Theological Seminary of America, 1956.

A collection of lectures and addresses by such notables as David Ben Gurion, Abba Eban, and Martin Buber divided into four sections: The role of Israel in the modern world; What history teaches; The new state; America and Israel.

FISHMAN, A.
The Religious Kibbutz Movement: The Revival of the Jewish Religious Community
New York: Zionist Organization, 1957.

A collection of essays providing an interesting account of the religious cooperative communities of Israel, with special emphasis on their religious aspects. The reader will especially enjoy the colorful vignettes of life in the kibbutz included in this work.

GOITEIN, S. D.
Jews and Arabs: Their Contact Through the Ages
New York: Schocken, 1955.

An historical account of the social and cultural contacts of the Jews and Arabs written by the Chairman of the School of Oriental Studies of the Hebrew University. The author's interpretation of the contemporary confrontation and belief that "during roughly the next twenty-five years, the two will become similar enough to make possible—if political conditions allow—neighborly relations..." is sure to stimulate thought and discussion.

HALPERN, B.
The Idea of the Jewish State
Cambridge, Mass.: Harvard University Press, 1961.

A significant historical study of the development of Zionism and the idea of the Jewish state and its reformulations to meet internal and external approval and support.

*HERTZBERG, A., editor
The Zionist Idea: A Historical Analysis and Reader
Cleveland: Meridian, 1960.

An excellent anthology of the Zionist literature of the 19th and 20th centuries with an introductory essay on Zionism by the editor. Included are selections of such authors as Hess, Herzl, Nordau, Ahad Ha-am, Kook, Buber, Brandeis, Weizmann, and Ben Gurion.

HERZL, T. (foreword by C. Weizmann)
The Jewish State: An Attempt at a Modern Solution of the Jewish Question
Jerusalem: Scopus Publishing Company, 1954.

"By the side of penetrating social and psychological analysis expressed with sparkling, aphoristic brilliance there are almost incredibly naive, utterly unnecessary, elaborate plans for the organization of the emigration from the Diaspora and the institutions, laws, and even manners of the future state."—C. Weizmann.

HESS, M. (translated from the German by M. J. Bloom)
Rome and Jerusalem
New York: Philosophical Library, 1958.

This 19th century classic in Zionist literature proposes a Jewish commonwealth in Palestine "in order to realize the historical ideal of our people, an ideal which is neither more nor less than the reign of God upon earth."

MEYER, I. S., editor
Early History of Zionism in America
New York: American Jewish Historical Society and Theodor Herzl Foundation, 1958.

A collection of seventeen papers on: Pre-Herzlian Zionism; The Writing of American Zionist History; The History of American Zionist Organizations; The Impact of Zionism on America.

*Book available in paperback edition.

PATAI, R.
Israel Between East and West: A Study of Human Relations
Philadelphia: Jewish Publication Society, 1953.

A scholarly study of the background and development of the social problems caused by the existence in Israel of two different major cultures and peoples—those of the Middle Eastern and European groups.

SAFRAN, N.
The United States and Israel
Cambridge: Harvard University Press, 1963.

A scholarly analysis of American and Israeli foreign relations published for the American Foreign Policy Library. This study also covers aspects of contemporary Israeli society.

*WEINGARTEN, M.
Life in a Kibbutz
New York: Recontructionist Press, 1955.

A native American vividly relates "the story of the kibbutz I helped found, describing the details of kibbutz organization and operation, and discussing the failings, advantages, and prospective development of kibbutz life."

XV. The Jews:
Their Internal Relations

BARKAI, M.
The Standard American Jewish Directory, 1960
New York: M. Barkai, 1960.

A valuable, comprehensive reference guide to the communal, religious and organizational life of the Jewish communities of the United States and Canada. Parts 1, 2 and 3 list, respectively: Congregations, Institutions and Organizations; Jewish Trades and Services; General Information.

BARON, S. W.
The Jewish Community: Its History and Structure to the American Revolution; 3 volumes
Philadelphia: Jewish Publication Society, 1942.

The classic, scholarly, historical account of the Jewish community focused on the European community of the Middle Ages and early modern times. Volume three provides approximately 570 pages of notes, bibliography, and index for the first two volumes.

CAHNMAN, W. J., editor
Intermarriage and Jewish Life: A Symposium
New York: Herzl Press and Reconstructionist Press, 1963.

A collection of papers by rabbis, Jewish educators, and social scientists on the problem of intermarriage. Included are essays entitled, "Intermarriage and the Survival of the Jewish People," "Intermarriage and Conversion on the American College Campus," and "Intermarriage Against the Background of American Democracy."

ENGELMAN, U. Z.
Hebrew Education in America: Problems and Solutions
New York: Jewish Teacher's Seminary and People's University Press, 1947.

This 62 page study of American Jewish education is part of the "Jewish Life in America" series. It traces the development of Jewish education from the "old world **heder**" to the "American Jewish weekday school" and discusses the problems involved in the transformation.

FEDERBUSH, S., editor
World Jewry Today
New York: Thomas Yoseloff, 1959.

An important reference work providing a concise account of the religious, economic, social, and political past and present of all the Jewish communities of the world —alphabetically arranged from Aden and Afghanistan through Yemen and Yugoslavia.

FISHMAN, I.
The History of Jewish Education in Central Europe from the End of the 16th Century to the End of the 18th Century
London: E. Goldston, 1944.

An important study of the nature and development of the Jewish educational system of Central Europe in the 17th and 18th centuries. This work discusses the private and communal schools, their organization, supervision, curriculum, and methods of teaching.

*Book available in paperback edition.

FRIEDMAN, T. and R. GORDIS, editors
Jewish Life in America
New York: Horizon Press, 1955.

An informative collection of essays dealing with the movements and forces of Jewish spiritual and cultural creativity in America.

GANNES, A. P.
Central Community Agencies for Jewish Education
Philadelphia: Dropsie College for Hebrew and Cognate Learning, 1954.

A study of the nature, growth, and development of the central community agencies for Jewish education since 1910. Includes a helpful bibliography on surveys and studies of Jewish education.

GOLDSTEIN, S. E.
The Synagogue and Social Welfare; A Unique Experiment (1907-1953)
New York: Bloch Publishing Company, 1955.

"In this volume...I have endeavored to describe the experiments we conducted in the Social Service Department of the Free Synagogue in order to meet community needs...to relate our experiences in selected areas of social action and the results achieved, and...to state what I believe to be the laws of social organization as derived from the experience, teachings and ideals of the Jewish people."—Author.

GORDON, A. I.
Jews in Suburbia
Boston: Beacon, 1959.

An interesting study of the religious and social problems faced by the American Suburban Jew. The reader will enjoy the sections on "The Jewish Family," "The Search For Religion," and "The Layer Community."

HOROWITZ, C. M. and L. J. KAPLAN
The Jewish Population of the New York Area 1900-1975
New York: Federation of Jewish Philanthropies, 1959.

A demographic study of the Jewish population of Greater New York from 1900 through 1958, and projected to 1975.

KATZ, J.
Tradition and Crisis
New York: Free Press, 1961.

A well written, authoritative examination of the internal Jewish communal structure of 16th and 17th century European Jewry from the sociological perspective.

KRAMER, J. R. and S. LEVENTMAN
Children of the Gilded Ghetto: Conflict Resolutions of Three Generations of American Jews
New Haven: Yale University Press, 1961.

A fine, readable sociological study of the Jewish community of North City, a midwestern American city typical and "reasonably representative of the minority situation of American Jews."

KURZWEIL, Z. E.
Modern Trends in Jewish Education
New York: Thomas Yoseloff, 1964.

A well-written, scholarly collection of essays pertaining to the history and philosophy of Jewish education during the last two hundred years.

LURIE, H. L.
A Heritage Affirmed
Philadelphia: Jewish Publication Society, 1961.

A well written discussion of the development, aims, programs, and organization of the Jewish federation movement in the United States and Canada from 1895 to the present time.

MAYER, J. E.
Jewish-Gentile Courtships, an Exploratory Study of a Social Process
New York: Free Press, 1961.

A sociological study of Jewish-Gentile courtships and the effects of the partners, parents, and friends in making the marital decision.

*SHERMAN, C. B.
The Jew Within American Society: A Study in Ethnic Individuality
Detroit: Wayne State University Press, 1961.

A sociological study of American Jewish life since the turn of the century with an emphasis on the uniqueness and individuality of the American Jew.

---

*Book available in paperback edition.

SKLARE, M., editor
The Jews: Social Patterns of an American Group
New York: Free Press, 1958.

    A collection of over thirty sociological studies of the contemporary American Jew. Included are sections on 1) The Jewish Community: Institutions, Social Patterns, Status, Structure, and Levels of Integration; and 2) The Jewish Religion: Aspects of Continuity and Change.

*ZBOROWSKI, M. and E. HERZOG
Life is With People: The Jewish Little Town of Eastern Europe
New York: International Universities Press, 1952.

    An anthropological and sociological study of the culture of the **shtetls,** the small town Jewish communities of Eastern Europe which existed until World War II.

XVI: The Jews:
Their External Relations

ADLER, C. and A. M. MARGALITH
With Firmness in the Right: American Diplomatic Action Affecting Jews, 1840-1945
New York: American Jewish Committee, 1946.

    An important collection of American diplomatic correspondence dealing with Jews. The work is divided into five parts: 1) the Near East and Morocco, 2) Rumania and Poland, 3) Russia, 4) Central Europe, and 5) the War Years, 1939-1945.

EPSTEIN, B. R. and A. FORSTER
Some of My Best Friends
New York: Farrar, Straus and Giroux, 1962.

    An account and analysis of the nature and extent of American anti-Semitism as evidenced by social discrimination and discrimination in housing, higher education and employment.

EPSTEIN, M.
The Jew and Communism: The Story of Early Communist Victories and Ultimate Defeats in the Jewish Community, U.S.A., 1919-1941
New York: Trade Union Sponsoring Committee, 1959.

    An objective survey of the impact and penetration of communism on the Jewish community in such areas as organized labor, war relief and rehabilitation, and the problems of Soviet Jewry.

FOERSTER, F. W.
The Jews
New York: Farrar, Straus and Giroux, 1962.

What the author describes as "a biology of the Hebrew mystery in the midst of the political history of peoples" is a touching and excellent account of the Jewish problem by a German Lutheran. His essays on "The Martyrology of Israel," "Jewish Faults and Their Causes," and "Christianity and Anti-Semitism" will prove interesting to the reader.

*HAY, M. V.
Europe and the Jews: The Pressure of Christendom on the People of Israel for 1900 Years
Boston: Beacon, 1960.

"A book he felt had to be done, and done by a Christian; a book admitting, exposing, examining, analyzing and condemning the 'chain of error' in Christian theology and Christian ethics which is called anti-Semitism."— From the introduction by Thomas Sugrue. (Originally published under the title: **The Foot of Pride.**)

*HERBERG, W.
Protestant, Catholic, Jew: An Essay in American Religious Sociology
Garden City: Doubleday, 1960.

A sociological study of the contemporary American religious societies and today's "upswing" in religion.

ISAAC, J. (translated from the French by H. Weaver)
The Teaching of Contempt: Christian Roots of Anti-Semitism
New York: Holt, Rinehart and Winston, 1964.

A gripping account of the Christian roots of anti-Semitism which the French-Jewish historian considers "the deepest ones of all." This work also contains the twenty-one propositions which the author propounded in his **Jesus et Israel.**

*KATZ, J.
Exclusiveness and Tolerance: Studies in Jewish-Gentile Relations in Medieval and Modern Times

*Book available in paperback edition.

New York: Oxford University Press, 1961.

A scholarly account of the changing attitudes of Ashkenazic Jewry towards their non-Jewish environment from the Middle Ages to the eighteenth century.

*LOEWENSTEIN, R. M.
Christians and Jews
New York: Delta, 1963.

"Dedicated to the Christians who gave their lives for persecuted Jews," this work is a brilliant psychoanalytic study of the causes and effects of anti-Semitism. The author maintains that "the historical role of Israel in the birth of Christianity was the mainspring of all anti-Semitic feelings..."

PARKES, J.
Anti-Semitism—A Concise World History
Chicago: Quadrangle, 1964.

Discusses group prejudice, psychology of prejudice, Christian roots of anti-Semitism, the anti-Semitic onslaught on Jews in the modern world, "the sterilization of prejudice."

*PARKES, J.
The Conflict of the Church and the Synagogue
Cleveland: World, 1961.

This classic study addresses itself to the problem: "Why was there a medieval ghetto?" Beginning with an account of the Jews in the Roman World, it traces Jewish relations with the pagan and Christian worlds into the beginning of the Middle Ages.

RAPHAEL, C.
Memoirs of a Special Case
Boston: Little, Brown, 1962.

The reader will gain an insight into the "special case" of being Jewish by reading the personal experiences of an important Jewish British statesman.

ROGOW, A. A.
The Jew in the Gentile World
New York: Macmillan, 1961.

An excellent anthology of writings about Jews by non-Jews from 419 B.C.E. through 1959 C.E. Each selection is prefaced by an introductory essay. Included are such authors as Apion, Tacitus, Saint Augustine, Martin Luther, Nietzsche, Hitler, Khrushchev, Mark Twain, Karl Meninger, and Reinhold Niebuhr.

SACHAR, A. L.
Sufferance is the Badge: The Jew in the Contemporary World
New York: Alfred A. Knopf, 1939.

An interesting study of the position of the Jew in Europe, the Middle East, and the United States from the end of World War I through events immediately preceding the outbreak of the second World War, in which he sees "the Hitlers and Mussolinis [as]... merely men of the moment who have pitted themselves against an enduring people."

SAMUEL, M.
The Great Hatred
New York: Alfred A. Knopf, 1940.

Published during World War II, this book emotionally addresses itself to the question: "How shall we begin to account for the mad disparity between the actual proportion of Jewish participation in contemporaneous Western life and the extent of the world's pre-occupation with the Jews?"

SARTRE, J. P. (translated from the French by G. J. Becker)
Anti-Semite and Jew
New York: Schocken, 1948; Grove, 1960.

A gripping series of essays on the problems of anti-Semitism, of which Sartre writes, "Anti-Semitism is a problem that affects us all directly... if we do not respect the person of the Israelite, who will respect us?"

*STEINBERG, M.
A Partisan Guide to the Jewish Problem
Indianapolis and New York: Bobbs-Merrill, 1945.

A study of the different faces of the "Jewish Problem," including "Problems of Status"; "Problems of Self-Acceptance"; "Problems of the Tradition;" and "Problems of the Homeland," which deals with the significance of Zionism and a Jewish homeland. (Written before the establishment of the State of Israel).

TELLER, J. L.
Scapegoat of Revolution
New York: Scribner's, 1954.

An interesting account of the effect of Socialism and Social Revolution on the Jews and anti-Semitism.

---

*Book available in paperback edition.

*TRACHTENBERG, J.
The Devil and the Jews; The Medieval Conception of the Jew and its Relation to Modern Anti-Semitism
Cleveland: World, 1961.

A revealing study of the medieval conception of the Jew and its bearing on the question: "How is it that men believe of the Jews what common sense would forbid them to believe of anyone else?" The work is divided into three parts: "The Demonic Jew," "The Jew as Sorcerer," and "The Jew as Heretic."

XVII. Biography

*FINKELSTEIN, L.
Akiba: Scholar, Saint and Martyr
Cleveland: World, 1962.

A penetrating, scholarly study of one who "ranks in depth of intellect, breadth of sympathy and clarity of vision with the foremost personalities in the Hebrew tradition...as he appears in the pages of the Talmud."

HERZL, T., edited by R. Patai (translated from the German by H. Zohn)
The Complete Diaries of T. Herzl; 5 volumes
New York: Herzl Press, 1960.

The complete diaries of the last nine years in the life of the founder of political Zionism in which he tirelessly worked to gain internal and external approval and acceptance of his movement.

Volume 5 is devoted to the notes and index for the first four volumes.

JUNG, L., editor
Guardians of Our Heritage (1724-1953)
New York: Bloch Publishing Company, 1958.

A collection of approximately thirty biographical essays on such notable figures as Isaac Leeser, Hirsch Hildesheimer, Avraham Kook, and Ezra Munk

MARCUS, J. R.
Memoirs of American Jews 1775-1865; 3 volumes
Philadelphia: Jewish Publication Society, 1955.

An anthology of the autobiographies, letters, and diaries of forty American Jews including Uriah Levy, Rebecca Gratz, and Oscar Straus. Each selection is prefaced by brief introductory remarks by the editor.

MARX, A.
Essays in Jewish Biography
Philadelphia: Jewish Publication Society, 1947.

Includes twelve biographies of figures such as Rabbenu Gershom, Rashi, Maimonides, David Hoffmann, Solomon Schechter and Max Margolis.

NOVECK, S., editor
Great Jewish Personalities in Ancient and Medieval Times
Washington, D.C.: B'nai B'rith Department of Adult Jewish Education, 1959.

An interesting collection of essays by important Jewish scholars of our day, on such figures as Moses, Jeremiah, Akiba, Saadia, Rashi, the Baal Shem Tov, and Vilna Gaon.

NOVECK, S., editor
Great Jewish Personalities in Modern Times
Washington, D. C.: B'nai B'rith Department of Adult Jewish Education, 1960.

A collection of eleven biographical essays on such important Jewish personalities as Mendelssohn, Montefiore, Solomon Schechter, Louis Brandeis, and Henrietta Szold.

NOVECK, S., editor
Great Jewish Thinkers of the Twentieth Century
Washington, D.C.: B'nai B'rith Department of Adult Jewish Education, 1963.

Ten biographical essays on such East European, German and American figures as Aaron Gordon, Leo Baeck, Kaufmann Kohler, Mordecai Kaplan, and Joseph Soloveitchik.

*SCHWARZ, L.
Memoirs of My People Through a Thousand Years
Philadelphia: Jewish Publication Society, 1943.

A broad selection of the diaries, memoirs, and letters of Jews from the 11th century to the present. Included are the writing of such notables as Moses Maimonides, Don Isaac Abravanel, Uriel da Costa, H. N. Bialik, and I. M. Wise.

*Book available in paperback edition.

SIMON, L.
Ahad Ha-Am (Asher Ginzberg): A Biography
Philadelphia: Jewish Publication Society, 1960.

A clear account of the life and thought of an ardent prophet and Zionist who believed "in the existence of a link between its [Israel's] national destiny and the ultimate triumph of righteousness on earth."

SIMONHOFF, H.
Saga of American Jewry 1865-1914; Links of an Endless Chain
New York: Arco Publishing Co., 1959.

A companion volume to **"Jewish Notables in America 1776-1865,"** this work also provides a brief biographical essay on "the outstanding Jew of each year." Included in this volume are essays on Moses Dropsie, Emma Lazarus, Samuel Gompers, Felix Adler, Adolph Ochs, Judah Magnes, and Oscar Hammerstein.

STEINBERG, M.
As a Driven Leaf
Indianapolis and New York: Bobbs-Merrill Co., 1939.

An historical, intellectual novel of the conflict between Hellenism and Rabbinic Judaism in the second century C. E. Deals with leaders of the Sanhedrin.

XVIII. Music and Art

BEN-ARI, R. (translated from the Hebrew by A. H. Gross and I. Soref)
Habima
New York: Thomas Yoseloff, 1957.

A well written account of the founding and development of the Habima, the Hebrew national theater, relating the "sacrifices, self-discipline and almost religious fervor, artistic and national, necessary to accomplish such a task."

*BERK, F., editor
The Jewish Dance: An Anthology of Articles
New York: Exposition Press, 1960.

A collection of five brief essays, which include "The Beginning of Jewish Dancing," "The Chassidic Dance," "Israel Dances," and "Jewish Dance Activities in America."

IDELSOHN, A. Z.
Jewish Music
New York: Tudor, 1948.
"The aim of this book is to give a description and an analysis of the elements and characteristics of Jewish music in their historical development."—Preface. A classic in this field.

KAYSER, S. S., editor
Jewish Ceremonial Art, second edition
Philadelphia: Jewish Publication Society, 1959.
"A guide to the appreciation of the art objects used in synagogue and home, principally from the collections of the Jewish Museum of the Jewish Theological Seminary of America."

LANDSBERGER, F.
A History of Jewish Art
New York: Union of American Hebrew Congregations, 1946.
This work, divided into two parts, deals with: 1) the role of art in Jewish life, in the synagogue and home; and 2) an historical survey of Jewish art from its beginnings through the present.

NAMENYI, E.
The Essence of Jewish Art
New York: Thomas Yoseloff, 1960.
An interesting study of the "key ideas that have dominated the many expressions of Jewish art in the course of eighteen centuries..."—God, the Chosen People, Torah, and Messianic Faith.

RABINOVITCH, I. (translated from the Yiddish by A. M. Klein)
Of Jewish Music, Ancient and Modern
New York: Bloch Publishing Co., 1952.
Among the many subjects discussed are: "Our Liturgic Song," "Chassidic Song," "The Pioneers and Creators of Modern Jewish Music," "Ernest Bloch," and "Jewish Music in America." Includes 28 musical illustrations.

*Book available in paperback edition.

ROTH, C., editor
Jewish Art, An Illustrated History
New York: McGraw-Hill, 1961.

An excellent collection of essays by nineteen distinguished individuals on Jewish Art from antiquity through modern times. Contains over 450 illustrations.

SCHWARZ, K.
Jewish Artists of the 19th and 20th Centuries
New York: Philosophical Library, 1949.

Intended "to define the respective position of the Jew in art by identifying him with his surroundings," this work provides the reader with a survey of the outstanding Jewish artists of the last 150 years (Antokolsky, Pissarro, Liebermann, Epstein, Chagall, etc.).

WERNER, E.
The Sacred Bridge
New York: Columbia University Press, 1959.

This scholarly work bears a self-explanatory subtitle: "The interdependence of liturgy and music in synagogue and church during the first millenium." This book is divided into two parts: 1) Historic-liturgical, and 2) Musical comparisons and studies.

WISCHNITZER, R.
Architecture of the European Synagogue
Philadelphia: Jewish Publication Society, 1964.

The history of European synagogue architecture from the Temple-oriented synagogue of Roman times down to the present day.

WISCHNITZER, R.
Synagogue Architecture in the U.S.; History and Interpretation
Philadelphia: Jewish Publication Society, 1955.

Devoted to a study of the architecture of the 19th and 20th century synagogues, this work displays "an extraordinary slice through the geologic layers, as it were, of our [American] architectural heritage." Contains over 150 illustrations.

Appendix A

PARTIAL LISTING OF PUBLIC, UNIVERSITY, AND JEWISH SPONSORED LIBRARIES WHERE THESE WORKS ARE OBTAINABLE.

California

University of Judaism Library
6525 Sunset Blvd.
Los Angeles, California

University of California Library
405 Hilgard Avenue
Los Angeles 24, California

Connecticut

Yale University Library
Curator of Hebrew—Dr. Leon Nemoy
New Haven, Connecticut

Illinois

The College of Jewish Studies Leaf Libraries
72 East 11th Street
Chicago 5, Illinois

The Hebrew Theological College Library
7135 Carpenter Road
Skokie, Illinois

Massachusetts

Boston Public Library
West End Branch
131 Cambridge Street
Boston 14, Massachusetts

Brandeis University Library
South Street
Waltham 54, Massachusetts

Harvard University Library
Cambridge 38, Massachusetts

Hebrew Teachers College Library
43 Hawes Street
Brookline, Massachusetts

New York

Hebrew Union College—
Jewish Institute of Religion Library

40 West 68th Street
New York 23, New York

Jewish Culture Foundation Library
New York University
2 North Washington Square
New York 3, New York

The Jewish Theological Seminary Library
3080 Broadway
New York 27, New York

New York Public Library
Jewish Division
42nd Street & 5th Avenue
New York 18, New York

Yeshiva University
Mendel Gottesman Library
Amsterdam Ave. & 186th St.
New York 33, New York

Ohio

The Klau Library
Hebrew Union College—
Jewish Institute of Religion
3101 Clifton Avenue
Cincinnati 20, Ohio

The Temple Library
E. 105 at Ansel Road
Cleveland 6, Ohio

Pennsylvania

Dropsie College for Hebrew & Cognate Learning Library
Broad & York Streets
Philadelphia 32, Pennsylvania

Free Library of Philadelphia
Logan Square
Philadelphia, Pennsylvania

Appendix B

JEWISH PERIODICALS (FREQUENCY OF PUBLICATION
AND SPONSORING ORGANIZATION ARE LISTED).

American Jewish Archives
3101 Clifton Avenue
Cincinnati 20, Ohio
Semi-annual. American Jewish Archives

American Jewish Historical Quarterly
150 Fifth Avenue
New York 11, New York
Quarterly. American Jewish Historical Society

CCAR Journal
790 Madison Avenue
New York 21, New York
Quarterly. Central Conference of American
Rabbis (Reform)

Commentary
165 East 56 Street
New York 22, New York
Monthly. American Jewish Committee

Congress Bi-Weekly
15 East 84th St.
New York 28, New York
Fortnightly. American Jewish Congress

Conservative Judaism
3080 Broadway
New York 27, New York
Quarterly. Rabbinical Assembly of
America (Conservative)

Hadassah Magazine
65 East 52 Street
New York 22, New York
Monthly. Hadassah, The Women's Zionist
Organization of America

Jewish Frontier
45 East 17th Street
New York 3, New York
Monthly. Jewish Frontier Association

Jewish Heritage
1640 Rhode Island Avenue, N.W.
Washington 36, D. C.
Quarterly. B'nai B'rith Adult Jewish
Education

Jewish Quarterly Review
Broad and York Streets
Philadelphia 32, Penna.
Quarterly. Dropsie College for Hebrew
and Cognate Learning

Jewish Social Studies
1841 Broadway
New York 23, New York
Quarterly. Conference on Jewish
Social Studies

Judaism
15 East 84th Street
New York 28, New York
Quarterly. American Jewish Congress

Midstream
515 Park Avenue
New York 22, New York
Quarterly. Theodor Herzl Foundation

National Jewish Monthly
1640 Rhode Island Avenue, N.W.
Washington 36, D. C.
Monthly. B'nai B'rith

The Reconstructionist
15 West 86th St.
New York 24, New York
Fortnightly. Jewish Reconstructionist
Foundation

Tradition
84 Fifth Avenue
New York 11, New York
Semi-annual. Rabbinical Council of
America (Orthodox)

Appendix C

PUBLISHERS OF BOOKS LISTED

Abelard-Schuman Ltd.
6 West 57 Street
New York, N.Y. 10019

American Biblical Encyclopedia Society
210 West 91 Street
New York, N.Y.

American Jewish Committee
165 East 56 Street
New York, New York

American Jewish Historical Society
150 Fifth Avenue
New York, N.Y. 10011

Anti-Defamation League
315 Lexington Avenue
New York, N.Y. 10016

Arco Publishing Co., Inc.
219 Park Avenue, S.
New York, N.Y. 10003

Atheneum Publishers
162 East 38 Street
New York, N.Y. 10016

Beacon Press
25 Beacon Street
Boston, Mass. 02108

Behrman House, Inc.
1261 Broadway
New York, N.Y. 10001

Bloch Publishing Co., Inc.
31 West 31 Street
New York, N.Y. 10001

B'nai B'rith Department of Adult
Jewish Education
1640 Rhode Island Avenue, N. W.
Washington, D. C. 20036

B'nai B'rith Hillel Foundation
1640 Rhode Island Avenue, N. W.
Washington, D. C. 20036

Bobbs-Merrill Co., Inc.
4300 West 62 Street
Indianapolis, Ind. 46206

George Braziller, Inc.
215 Park Avenue, S.
New York, N.Y. 10003

Broadman Press
127 Ninth Avenue, N.
Nashville, Tenn. 37203

Burning Bush Press
2852 Broadway
New York, N.Y. 10025

Central Book Co., Inc.
850 DeKalb Avenue
Brooklyn, N.Y.

Citadel Press
222 Park Avenue, S.
New York, N.Y. 10003

Clarendon Press
417 Fifth Avenue
New York, N.Y. 10016

Columbia University Press
2960 Broadway
New York, N.Y. 10027

Compass Books
625 Madison Avenue
New York, N.Y. 10022

Cornell University Press
124 Roberts Place
Ithaca, N.Y. 14851

Crown Publishers, Inc.
419 Park Avenue, S.
New York, N.Y. 10016

Delta Books
750 Third Avenue
New York, N.Y. 10017

Devin-Adair Co.
23 East 26 Street
New York, N.Y. 10010

Doubleday and Co., Inc.
277 Park Avenue
New York, N.Y. 10017

Dover Publications, Inc.
180 Varick Street
New York, N.Y. 10014

Dropsie College for Hebrew
and Cognate Learning
Broad and York Streets
Philadelphia 32, Pa.

E. P. Dutton and Co., Inc.
201 Park Avenue, S.
New York, N.Y. 10003

*Dvir Co. Ltd.
58 Maze
Tel Aviv, Israel

East and West Library
(Jewish Publication Society of America)
222 North 15 Street
Philadelphia, Pa. 19102

Exposition Press
386 Park Avenue, S.
New York, N.Y. 10016

Farrar, Straus and Giroux
19 Union Square, W.
New York, N.Y. 10003

Fortress Press
2900 Queen Lane
Philadelphia, Pa. 19129

Federation of Jewish Philanthropies
130 East 59 Street
New York, N.Y.

Free Press of Glencoe, Inc.
640 Fifth Avenue
New York, N.Y. 10019

Funk and Wagnalls Co., Inc.
360 Lexington Avenue
New York, N.Y. 10017

**E. Goldston, Ltd.
London, England
(No known address)

Grove Press
64 University Place
New York, N.Y. 10003

Walter D. E. Gruyter & Co.
West Berlin 30
Republic of West Germany

Harcourt, Brace and World, Inc.
757 Third Avenue
New York, N.Y. 10017

Harper and Row, Publishers
49 East 33 Street
New York, N.Y. 10016

Harvard University Press
79 Garden Street
Cambridge, Mass. 02138

Hebrew Publishing Co.
79 Delancey Street
New York, N.Y.

Hebrew Union College Press
239 Park Avenue, S.
New York, N.Y. 10003

Herzl Press
515 Park Avenue
New York, N.Y. 10022

Holt, Rinehart and Winston, Inc.
383 Madison Avenue
New York, N.Y. 10017

Horizon Press
156 Fifth Avenue
New York, N.Y. 10010

International Universities Press, Inc.
227 West 13 Street
New York, N.Y. 10011

Jewish Book Council of America
145 East 32 Street
New York, N.Y. 10016

**Jewish Chronicle Publications
37 Furnival Street
London, England

Jewish Education Committee Press
426 West 58 Street
New York, N.Y. 10019

Jewish Encyclopedic Handbooks
25 East 78 Street
New York, N.Y.

Jewish Publication Society of America
222 North 15 Street
Philadelphia, Pa. 19102

Jewish Teacher's Seminary and People's
University Press
515 Park Avenue
New York, N.Y.

Jewish Theological Seminary of America
3080 Broadway
New York, N.Y. 10027

Jonathan David, Publishers, Inc.
131 East 23 Street
New York, N.Y. 10010

Alfred A. Knopf, Inc.
501 Madison Avenue
New York, N.Y. 10022

Ktav Publishing House, Inc.
47 Canal Street
New York, N.Y. 10002

Little, Brown and Company
34 Beacon Street
Boston, Mass. 02106

The Macmillan Co.
60 Fifth Avenue
New York, N.Y. 10011

*Magnes Press
Hebrew University
Jerusalem, Israel

McGraw-Hill Book Company
330 West 42 Street
New York, N.Y. 10036

David McKay Co., Inc.
750 Third Avenue
New York, N.Y. 10017

Mentor Books
501 Madison Avenue
New York, N.Y. 10022

Meridian
2231 West 110 Street
Cleveland, Ohio 44102

**Mishna Press, Ltd.
5 Darthout Park Hill
London, England

Modern Library, Inc.
457 Madison Avenue
New York, N.Y. 10022

Thomas Nelson and Sons
Copewood and Davis Streets
Camden, N.J. 08103

**Oliver and Boyd, Ltd.
39 Welbeck Street
London, England

Oxford University Press, Inc.
417 Fifth Avenue
New York, N.Y. 10016

Pardes Publishing House, Inc.
120 East Broadway
New York, N.Y.

Penguin Books, Inc.
3300 Clipper Mill Road
Baltimore, Md. 21211

Philosophical Library, Inc.
15 East 40 Street
New York, N.Y. 10016

Prentice-Hall, Inc.
Englewood Cliffs, N. J. 07632

Princeton University Press
Princeton, N. J. 08541

Quadrangle Books, Inc.
180 North Wacker Drive
Chicago, Ill. 60606

Random House
457 Madison Avenue
New York, N.Y. 10022

Reconstructionist Press
15 West 86 Street
New York, N.Y. 10024

Rutgers University Press
30 College Avenue
New Brunswick, N. J. 08903

Schocken Books, Inc.
67 Park Avenue
New York, N.Y. 10016

*Scopus Publishing Co.
Jerusalem, Israel
(Address unknown)

Charles Scribner's Sons
597 Fifth Avenue
New York, N.Y. 10017

**Shapiro, Vallentine and Co.
81 Wentworth Street
London, England

Soncino Press, Ltd.
84 Fifth Avenue
New York, N.Y. 10011

Syracuse University Press
University Station
Syracuse 10, New York

Peter Smith
20 Railroad Avenue
Gloucester, Mass. 01930

Trade Union Sponsoring Committee
22 West 38 Street
New York, N.Y. 10018

Tudor Publishing Co.
221 Fourth Avenue
New York, N.Y. 10003

Twayne Publishers, Inc.
31 Union Square, W.
New York, N.Y. 10003

UNESCO Publications Center
317 East 34 Street
New York, N.Y.

Union of American Hebrew Congregations
838 Fifth Avenue
New York, N.Y. 10021

Universal Jewish Encyclopedia Co.
(No longer in existence)

University of Chicago Press
5750 Ellis Avenue
Chicago, Ill. 60637

**University of London Press, Ltd.
Hodder and Stoughton, Ltd.
Warwick Lane
London, England

Viking Press
625 Madison Avenue
New York, N.Y. 10022

Washington Square Press, Inc.
630 Fifth Avenue
New York, N.Y. 10020

Wayne State University Press
5980 Cass
Detroit, Mich. 48202

Westminster Press
Witherspoon Building
Philadelphia, Pa. 19107

World Publishing Co.
2231 West 110 Street
Cleveland, Ohio 44102

Yale University Press
749 York Street
New Haven, Conn. 06511

Yivo'Institute for Jewish Research
1048 Fifth Avenue
New York, N.Y.

Thomas Yoseloff, Publisher
8 East 36 Street
New York, N.Y. 10016

Zionist Organization
Youth and Hechalutz Department
515 Park Avenue
New York, N.Y.

*An index of book stores from which these and other works listed here can be obtained, will be found in the **Standard American Jewish Directory.** (See page 50 of this bibliography.)

**All books published in London can be obtained at The British Book Centre, Inc., 122 East 55 Street, New York, N.Y.

INDEX